Innovations in Education Series
Edited by Robert J. Brown

1. Edward J. Dirkswager, editor. *Teachers as Owners: A Key to Revitalizing Public Education*. 2002.
2. Darlene Leiding. *The Won't Learners: An Answer to Their Cry*. 2002.
3. Ronald J. Newell. *Passion for Learning: How a Project-Based System Meets the Needs of High School Students in the 21st Century*. 2003.
4. Sarah J. Noonan. *The Elements of Leadership: What You Should Know*. 2003.
5. Jeffrey R. Cornwall. *From the Ground Up: Entrepreneurial School Leadership*. 2003.
6. Linda Schaak Distad and Joan Cady Brownstein. *Talking Teaching: Implementing Reflective Practice in Groups*. 2004.
7. Darlene Leiding. *Managers Make the Difference: Managing vs. Leading in Our Schools*. 2004.

Managers Make the Difference

Managing vs. Leading in Our Schools

Darlene Leiding

ScarecrowEducation
Lanham, Maryland • Toronto • Oxford
2004

Published in the United States of America
by ScarecrowEducation
An imprint of The Rowman & Littlefield Publishing Group, Inc.
4501 Forbes Boulevard, Suite 200, Lanham, Maryland 20706
www.scarecroweducation.com

PO Box 317
Oxford
OX2 9RU, UK

British Library Cataloguing in Publication Information Available

Library of Congress Cataloging-in-Publication Data

Leiding, Darlene, 1943–
  Managers make the difference : managing vs. leading in our
schools / Darlene Leiding.
      p. cm. — (Innovations in education series ; 7)
  Includes bibliographical references and index.
  ISBN 1-57886-138-1 (pbk. : alk. paper)
  1. Educational leadership—United States. 2. School
management and organization—United States. 3. School
improvement programs—United States. I. Title. II. Series.
LB2805.L3354 2004
371.2—dc22

                                          2004001025

⊚™ The paper used in this publication meets the minimum requirements of
American National Standard for Information Sciences—Permanence of Paper
for Printed Library Materials, ANSI/NISO Z39.48-1992.
Manufactured in the United States of America.

Contents

Introduction

There are three kinds of groups: those that make things happen, those that wait for things to happen, and those that wonder what happened.

—Anonymous

Many problems face us: hunger, homelessness, pollution, budget deficits, urban decay, arts under attack, medical costs, and medical coverage. Violence plagues the country, and prisons have not lowered crime rates. Businesses need to be more competitive while unions struggle with their role. Entry-level jobs require critical thinking skills, yet schools are faced with mounting social problems that hinder education. Government demands compliance to a host of separate rules, and foundations fund mostly individual programs for one to two years, leaving them to scramble for additional resources.

All of these problems are interrelated. Thus we need to address the common sources of the problems rather than waiting to fix separate symptoms. We need to think of long-term changes as well as short-term actions. No one person or group alone can confront our problems for long.

Individually, good people and organizations are agreeing to do something about these problems. But we live in a highly interrelated global society, and actions within a single sector affect many other sectors in many other places. Furthermore, each of these places has its own stakeholders.

Bringing together diverse stakeholders, melding their resources, and stretching their minds to embrace new ideas and a new language is essential to resolving problems facing our schools. Leadership intertwined with management provides an opportunity and a challenge to bring people together. The process becomes a continuing phenomenon that empowers people and systems to change.

> People deal too much with the negative, with what is wrong. . . . Why not try and see positive things, to just touch those things and make them bloom?
>
> —Thech Nhat Hanh

Unless public schools become the architects of change, we fear they will become the victims of change. A sense of urgency about educational difficulties in the United States permeates conversations about education in the media, statehouse, community, and classroom. No one buys the idea that because our schools face daunting challenges, the nation needs to scale back its ambitions for educating youth.

Schools are challenged by an enrollment boom, limited institutional flexibility, new competition for students, eroding public trust, a graying teaching force, growing numbers of immigrant and poor children, and troubling evidence about institutional effectiveness.

We have run out of easy solutions. The road on our journey is not straight, but twists and turns. Adding a program here, squeezing in more teachers there, increasing funding slightly—these and other strategies no longer work.

Issues remain:

- What should be taught?
- How can performance be improved?
- What do students need to know?
- Who should teach?
- Education for whom? (school desegregation, bilingual education, multicultural education, education for children with disabilities)
- How should schools be run? (school reform, school restructuring)
- How should education be financed?

In his book *Leadership for the Schoolhouse*, Thomas Sergiovanni (1996, 107) says that school leaders should help their institutions strive to become "purposeful communities, caring communities, inquiring communities, and respectful communities that are able to function successfully in a democratic society." To forge agreements, or what Sergiovanni calls covenants, on a school's shared values, ideals, and purposes, he recommends that school leaders ask these questions of teachers, students, parents, and others in the school community:

- What do we want students to become?
- What do we want students to think?
- What do we want students to reason?
- What do we want students to value and believe?
- How can we help students become persons of character in our democratic society?
- How do we want students to work together, inquire together, and learn together?
- What is our role as educators?
- What are our responsibilities?
- How can we work together as adults?
- How will we share leadership in this school?
- Is there a role for managers?

Kids aren't widgets. Schools are places where the human heart is as important as the human mind.

Educators need to "invent their own practice." Creating a theory of school leadership and management involves adopting a "mindscape," an all-encompassing perspective that includes the entire school landscape from the science laboratory to the cafeteria, and from the bus stop to the business office.

Schools should be aesthetically pleasing, offering beautiful images and language that nurture children and teachers. Schools should be democratic and emphasize moral connections, which means taking responsibility for one's actions and doing the right thing. Schools are first and foremost learning communities and must be carefully led and managed.

We are facing tremendous change and heated competition. We are facing cutbacks and downsizing. We may still be smarting from the last round of reengineering and reinvention. Ringing in our ears are the demands to do more with less and work smarter, not harder. We have tried solutions that used to work, such as smaller class sizes, smaller schools, and more teachers, but those solutions just aren't enough anymore. The problems, or what we think are the problems, have changed.

The only competitive edge we have is how we harness the creative energy of the people who work with us and for us to develop new approaches to problems and implement solutions that work.

How do you work smarter? How do you do more with less? How do you create new approaches and creative solutions to difficult problems?

This book will deliver practical methods you can apply to help your school become more creative and nurture the creativity in the teachers and staff.

Our goal is to achieve results. This book focuses on results. Creativity for creativity's sake is great, and it can be a lot of fun, but in today's educational world we need to achieve significant results at a much faster pace than at any other time in history.

Over the course of my career I have found that educational organizations are 90 percent the same. The high percentage of similarity derives from the fact that all educational organizations are composed of a group of people who are *hopefully* working together toward a common goal. I emphasize "hopefully" because many times people are *not* working toward a common goal. Many times they do not even know what the goal is.

The educational organization that will survive and thrive in the twenty-first century will not be the one with the deepest pockets, but the one that can unleash and apply the creativity of the workforce and the schools—the one with leaders and managers who recognize and take steps to promote such creativity.

> The greatest threat to any organization is not the lack of ability or resources, but the failure of imagination.
>
> —David Meier, Center for Accelerated Learning.

If things are going well in your school—if people are invested in their work, contributing ideas and moving students forward, and think their school is a great place to work—there is a 67 percent chance you are doing some things right.

On the other hand, if staff are not involved in the life of the school—if they loathe their jobs and think their school is a wretched place to work—there is a 67 percent chance it is your fault.

Leaders: The cold, hard truth is that your behavior is the single most important factor in determining whether the people who work for you will be creative. A beautiful new building means nothing if you do not support your staff in developing their ideas and implementing new approaches for solving problems. You must lead and manage.

As Bernard Bass (1999, 283) summarizes: "Leaders manage and managers lead, but the two are not synonymous. . . . Management functions can potentially provide leadership; leadership can contribute to managing. Nevertheless, some managers do not lead, and some leaders do not manage." Leadership and management overlap but they are not the same. Since the distinction is not always clear throughout our society it should come as no surprise that we are not clear about management and leadership in education either.

Warren Bennis (1999, 9), popular writer of leadership resources and business professor at the University of Southern California in Los Angeles, shares the same view. "There is a profound difference between management and leadership, and both are important. To manage means to bring about, to accomplish, to have charge of or responsibility for, to conduct. Leading is influencing, guiding in a direction, course, and action and having an opinion. The distinction is crucial." One of Bennis's most quoted phrases is, "Managers are people who do things right, and leaders are people who do the right thing."

Leadership and management are both important, but they seek to do different things. Every educational program structures itself to accomplish its goals in a way that is in tune with or responsive to its environment. Once the efficiency of the program is established, educators simply go about maintaining the system, assuming that the environment will stay the same. Management is the main focus because it keeps the program going well with little change. But the thing is, the environment for any educational organization is always changing. There are always shifts in educational trends, social attitudes, society's culture, technology, historical events, and so forth. The world is not static as we assume. Educational organizations tend not to spot these changes quickly, often because of a "management orientation" that is focused more on "looking in" instead of "looking out." Over time, schools can become less and less in tune with or responsive to the environment, creating more and more management problems.

Times like this require schools to think more in terms of leadership. Leaders begin to ask questions like, "What is really going on here?" "How do we become relevant again?" "How do we fulfill our goals in these new times?" "What will prompt parents to think what we do is meaningful?" Leaders seek to bring schools more in line with the realities of their environment, which often necessitates changing the very structures, resources, and leadership that they have worked so long and so hard to manage. Leaders can bring renewed vitality to their staff.

Educational leaders need to ask themselves, every so often, whether they are really leaders or managers. They need to ask questions like:

- What is changing in our communities?
- Are we being responsible?
- What is no longer working in our school the way it did a few years ago? Why is this the case?
- In the long run, what is really important for the future of this school?

As we explore management and leadership we must be careful of signs of "inbred management"—people who are so entrenched in the habitual practices of handling the school organization that they are incapable of innovation, change, or even of maintaining organizational health. Their focus is so captured by routine that their ability to appreciate the bigger picture is hampered. The following are six signs of inbred management:

- People cling to old ways of working even though they are confronted by a new situation.
- New goals that have meaning and challenge are not defined.
- Action is taken without studied reflection. Behavior is rooted in tradition rather than need.
- Institutionalized contentment exists; activity is secure and stable, not venturesome.
- Old "wisdom" is passed on to new people. Older managers tend to adhere to old ideas and antiquated approaches and methods.
- Low tolerance for criticism acts to stifle independent thinking.

Every school tends toward these characteristics. The question is, "How much is your school dominated by them?"

Many schools are in dire circumstances that cannot be addressed in traditional ways. Major restructuring efforts are being undertaken by school districts due to the nature of the problems they face and their resistance to traditional solutions. Serious attempts to restructure schools seek to alter the fundamental ways in which schools operate, in areas of either curriculum or governance, with the hope of improving student learning. Those involved in reform efforts are aware of the complexity of school problems and the resistance of schools to change efforts.

The reform movement places emphasis on the value and importance of leadership and management in our schools. Although the literature about effective schools stresses the importance of top administrative leadership, educators have come to understand how more diverse, school-based management can help make school improvement a reality.

Leaders are people oriented, whereas managers are task oriented. Leaders inspire, managers organize. Sometimes it is difficult to distinguish when you are leading and when you are managing. All of us have objectives and tasks to perform, and this requires planning, organizing, and directing; but the overwhelming task is the people. They must be found, hired, trained, organized, and applied to the task, which is what managing is all about. Certainly, people are a resource that must be applied in a planned and organized way, but they must also be inspired and motivated—they must be led.

People represent a very large variable in all situations because they can be completely unpredictable. Some will resign to go surfing, others will demand unscheduled time off; quarrels will develop, and unfortunately, health issues can impact any situation. The job of managing people is a combination of an opera impresario, a counselor, and a drill sergeant.

We need to realize that in the world of managing and leadership there is no single answer. Human beings and human events are unpredictable. Therefore the effective leader must look at every situation from different perspectives and be prepared to react to changing circumstances, behavior, and unanticipated events. I am not sure there is ever any one answer to management or leadership problems; only the participants can determine the one best suited for their situation.

How to manage and lead effectively has been the subject of many books and articles. Educators have labored over this question, managers have documented their experiences, and droves of consultants have coached from the sidelines. Yet this question remains open, and a visit to any bookstore finds shelf after shelf of books devoted to this subject. After all of these years of research and experience, why do we not know how to manage and lead effectively?

Management and leadership have been with us since the beginning of civilization. So have processes and procedures. There has always been the right way, the wrong way, and "my" way of doing something. This attitude of self-assurance is so prevalent that it is virtually part of our culture.

Schools today provide a laboratory for reviewing issues of reform and educational choice. They represent teacher-designated educational programs. In order to operate successfully these schools need leadership and management.

My expertise over the past ten years has been in the alternative school and charter school movements. I have had the privilege of helping start a charter school from the weeks prior to opening and then serving as its principal for two years. I left for other challenges after the charter school was able to stand on its own.

I was given the honor of creating an alternative school from the drawing board to fruition. This is a principal's dream . . . to create a school that will help all students succeed. Again I left for new challenges when the CEO took the school in a direction I could not agree with.

Everything that I believe in about education was severely tested in my latest challenge. I was named principal of a culturally diverse charter school that the State Department of Education was about to close because of noncompliance in several areas, as well as for financial mismanagement.

The school had no organized financial system. There was no budget and the previous administration was spending money that they did not have. Special education was noncompliant due to improper assessing procedures, and qualifications were not following federal guidelines. Individual Education Plans (IEPs) were written incorrectly. Food and nutrition funds were mismanaged. Test scores of the students were well below the state's and sponsoring district's norms. In fact, the test scores went down every year, not up. The longer children remained in school, the worse they scored. Several of the teaching staff did not possess valid teaching licenses.

I have discovered over the past two years that I must be both a manager and a leader. As a manager I had to terminate seventeen staff and take a long, hard look at the facts and the issues. As a leader, I had to "lead" the school in a new direction if we were to survive. There were a multitude of issues that I had to address. Finances were really a disaster, the media was not friendly, accountability was a foreign word, and few inside and outside the school could demonstrate understanding.

Unfortunately many schools across the nation are having difficulty because of similar issues and problems. What can be done?

This book will enable readers to learn how to handle similar situations in their schools.

Chapter 1 covers a brief history of education in the United States. To move forward we must look to the past. Education was important to the citizens of colonial America. The colonial period, common school period, progressive period, and modern period are discussed in this chapter.

Chapter 2 addresses the difference between management and leadership. School administrators are expected to lead with a vision in mind supported by long-range planning and at the same time manage the day-to-day operation of the school. The manager rules, the leader is followed.

Chapter 3 covers the current status of our nation's schools, good and bad school boards, school report cards, and the conscience and ethics of American youth.

Chapter 4 investigates finances. How schools can budget and even save money is the focus. Plugging into energy savings, energy conservation, covering construction costs, and strategies for avoiding financial disaster are discussed.

Chapter 5 covers accountability.

Chapter 6 lets teachers speak for themselves. What does it take to be a good teacher? How do we improve the quality of our teaching force? Why do teachers choose to teach?

Chapter 7 is entitled "The Media Monster." Educators must make communication a priority if they are to gain public support. Better ways of linking the schools and the community are also discussed.

Chapter 8 is about "The Awesome School." Awesome schools are neither educational panaceas nor fads. They allow educators to combine genuine diversity and cutting-edge innovation with rigorous standards and accountability. Creating and sustaining these schools under leadership and management is the focus of this chapter.

It has become a cliché to say that these are precarious times for public schools. It is also a reality. On the one hand, improving schools is the public's top priority. On the other, significant numbers of U.S. citizens are giving up on public schools. More people are willing to say "yes" to alternatives that include public vouchers for private and parochial schools, untested charter schools, and public schools operated by private firms.

Educators who work in our nation's schools represent the conscience of a society because they shape the conditions under which future generations learn about themselves and their relationship to others in the world.

Educators, families, and community members need to reinvigorate the language, social relations, and politics of our educational system. We must analyze how power shapes knowledge, and how education can help students reconcile the seemingly opposing needs of freedom and solidarity. As educators and interested stakeholders we need to examine alternative models of education that challenge the organization of public schools. Pioneering educators such as Deborah Meier, Ted Sizer, James Comer, and Joe Nathan, as well as groups like the Center for School Change, are working hard to link educational policies and classroom practices to expand the scope of freedom, justice, and democracy.

Americans must address the problems of public schooling in the realms of values and politics, while holding firm to the possibilities of public education in strengthening the practice of active citizenship. Schooling should enable students to involve themselves in the deepest problems of society, to acquire the knowledge, the skills, and the ethical vocabulary necessary for what the philosopher and former Czech president Vaclav Havel calls "the richest possible participation in public life" (1998, 45). Havel's comment suggests that educators must defend schools as essential to the life of the nation because schools are one of the few public spaces left where students can learn about and engage in the experience of democracy.

1

The History of Education in America

The future of mankind lies waiting
For those who come to understand their lives
And take up their responsibilities
To all living things.

—Vine Victor Deloria Jr., Standing Rock Sioux

To many Americans the term "colonial period" calls to mind a hodge-podge vision of Captain John Smith being saved by Pocahontas, of Pilgrims landing on Plymouth Rock and catching turkeys for Thanksgiving, of Peter Stuyvesant stomping angrily about New Amsterdam, of Indian Wars and scalping along the Mohawk valley, of the tea party in the Boston harbor, of Paul Revere riding through the night, of Washington at Valley Forge, and of the surrender of Cornwallis at Yorktown. The "colonial period" in this view is a romantic and picturesque subject appropriate primarily for story, fable, and song. To many Americans the "colonial period" is associated mainly with the first chapter of tedious textbooks in American history and a long series of now vaguely remembered dates, names, and events: Queen Anne's War, King George's War, the French and Indian War, the Quebec Act, the Sugar Act, the Stamp Act, the Tea Act, and the Declaration of Independence.

Let it be said at once that the intention of this chapter is to try neither to glamorize our remote past nor to repeat the usual formulas of chronological history. It is important, however, for anyone who would face realistically the current problems of American education to look again at the roots of our American traditions. The roots of some of our most controversial and urgent problems of the present are firmly imbedded in the colonial period. I will not deal exhaustively with all or even a large part of the colonial history that would be considered important by historians. I selected for this chapter those basic patterns that help to explain the education of the past and help to throw light upon the present. If we combine these interests and attempt to select those educational problems that were of greatest importance to the colonists in their own day and that remain of most importance to our day, we have a promising principle by which to select and organize our reexamination of American education.

Of all the present problems that have their roots in the colonial period, three stand out. First, American educators are arguing about the proper role of education in relation to the state; in the colonial period the distinctive American patterns of political and state authority were being hammered out. Second, the problem of the proper role of religion and education is still being debated; in the colonial period the seeds of our present controversies were being planted. Third, the merits of equality of educational opportunity as a present goal for American education are being hotly disputed; in the colonial period the basic patterns of economic class and sectional distinctions were being laid.

Looking at some more or less familiar historical material makes me believe that even old material looks new when looked at with the purpose of facing the important tasks of today. I hope that we can look at our history again with renewed interest spurred by the desire to untangle present confusions.

Education throughout the colonial period was a function of political sovereignty. Even where education was conducted by private or religious agencies, it was a grant of power by the political authority, whether king, proprietor, or colonial legislature. When the colonies became independent states, they assumed similar prerogatives in law. Without this fundamental tradition of political and state authority the states of the nineteenth century would have found it extremely difficult to extend public control over education or to establish the public systems of education that became so important a feature of American life.

As stated earlier, two other cultural patterns of the colonial period were of prime importance for education. One was the inherited alliance between church and state, which meant that the political authority could properly legislate on religious matters and on religious education. The changes and development that took place during the colonial period led to the separation of church and state in the Revolutionary and early national periods. The other was the pattern of economic class sectional relationships, which created serious problems and conflicts within the colonies and vitally influenced the kind of schooling and opportunity for education that developed in colonial times.

One of the oldest and most difficult problems is the relationship between religion and education. American educators have long debated whether religious instruction should be given in public schools and whether public funds should be allocated to religious schools. Questions such as these stir the emotions and elicit hot arguments on both sides.

The historical struggle for religious liberty was not only allied with the struggle for political democracy but was also involved in the struggle for social democracy. This raised the problem of conflict among economic interests, class differences, and sectional antagonisms, which acted as threat to and as seedbed for a growing democracy.

Americans have long been proud of their tradition of equality as well as their traditions of liberty and popular government. The American dream has been shaped by our belief that "all men are created equal," or at least that all people should be treated as though they have an equal opportunity to make of themselves what they will. This ideal has been the motivating force behind much of the humanitarian and reform movements that led to the abolition of slavery, universal suffrage, and universal free education. The actual conditions under which people lived and the changes they worked and fought for prompted a critical look at the kind of education that would be appropriate to the times. New outlooks on life caused educators to bring their ideas to bear upon educational goals, content, and practice.

Let us now take a brief walk through the history of education in America.

THE COLONIAL PERIOD (1600–1776)

In colonial America, particularly in New England, the first educational establishments were built for the purpose of teaching religion. After all, if kids couldn't read they couldn't read the Bible. There was also a need for a trained ministry. Education was so important to the citizens of colonial America that in 1647 the first law regarding education was inducted in Massachusetts. This law stated that if parents neglected to instruct their children, the state would take over the duty. Connecticut passed a similar law in 1650.

New England was also at the forefront of the advancement of higher education (Harvard University was founded in 1636). Courses were offered in theology, literature, arts, and science. William and Mary College was erected in 1693 in Williamsburg, Virginia, as was a combined seminary and college to cater to the needs of Virginia planters. However, many planters continued to send their sons to England for their education, especially those studying law.

In smaller communities, most teaching was provided by female members of the community church. Only the larger towns could afford a qualified master (manager) to run a grammar school, and these were restricted to boys. Outside New England, the diversity in religious attitudes created diversity in the schools. Most left the attainment of salvation to the guidance of a minister instead of to personal study by the individual. These elitist views were especially obvious in the Anglican Church. The Baptists and the Quakers cared the least about education, however, because they relied on inspiration and spontaneity, for which neither formal training nor literacy were necessary.

In these early days, it was only natural that the town meeting turned its attention to schools as well as to other political, economic, religious, and social matters. This early concern for education resulted in the establishment of town schools for the teaching of Latin grammar, the means by which boys could proceed to higher education and thus gain a liberal education appropriate for leadership in church and state.

The town authorities began by appointing a schoolmaster to open a school. The town would grant a parcel of public land for the building and support of a school. Most of the towns accepted as a matter of course that the schools thus set up should be under the management and supervision of the town authorities. The schools were "public schools" because they existed by authority of the town government. All parents had the right to send their children to them. However, they were not "public" because the parents who could afford to do so paid fees or tuitions, and arrangements for the education of the poor children were made in other ways than sending them to a Latin School.

In the middle and Southern colonies, schooling was left to individual parishes and communities. The middle colonies were characterized by schools sponsored by many different kinds of religious denominations. William Penn and Benjamin Franklin stressed practical education. There was an increased need for clerks and other literate working people. The wealthy decided that those who were educated were not only financially superior, but morally superior as well. Many towns set up free schools for the poorer students so they also would have a chance to become educated and thus enhance the moral and financial superiority of the new nation. The increase in schools led to an increase in those entering the teaching profession, which had now become accepted as a separate vocation from the ministry.

Southerners believed that education was a private matter and not a concern for the state. They were quick to point out that in all traditional societies the child receives the most important training in the home, where he or she is inducted into the values of the society he or she is about to enter. If the family fails in this endeavor, then how can the schools be successful? There were few schools in the South. Many of the plantation owners sent their male children abroad if they wanted formal schooling in the areas of Latin, the humanities, and the arts. Southerners felt a priority should be placed upon creating a college-bred elite, if their traditions and way of life were to be successfully transferred to successive generations. This system helped to perpetuate the sharply defined social-class structure that existed in the South. There were planters (plantation owners) and there were slaves; no middle class existed in the South to bridge the gap between upper and lower classes, and as such, there was no demand for services beyond those provided for families who could afford to pay.

Another reason that public education did not flourish in the South was that the population was more dispersed that it was in the North, making it difficult to find enough children in one area to justify a school.

Finally we must consider the South's feeling about slavery. "Knowledge is Power" was meant for the elite. Who should be entrusted with this power was a source of discussion: certainly, not a slave. Southern colonies began passing laws to make it a crime to teach slaves to read and write. Only the Catholics and Quakers continued their efforts to educate the black people in the South, and they were few in number. The religious leaders in the South supported the slave owner by providing oral (not written) religious training for slaves. One minister commented that instead of reading the Bible, literate slaves would soon be reading documents filtering down from the North inciting rebellion, and then pose a threat to the Southern family.

Children in both the North and the South were taught from an early age that mankind was divided naturally by race, each race having certain physical and mental characteristics that had remained fundamentally unchanged throughout history. The white race was at the top of the hierarchy and the black race was at the bottom. The white man was assigned the task of "civilizing and enlightening the world." A child influenced by this ongoing indoctrination would not expect the black race to take an equal place in American civilization. Southerners justified slavery on the basis that the black man was incapable of improvement, all the while denying them access to any type of formalized education. However, even in time of great adversity, education of the black people continued, often covertly conducted under the cover of night. The quest for knowledge could not be thwarted.

The school system in the 1700s put a much stronger emphasis on science than ever before. Students were beginning to find the traditional religious explanations of their environment unconvincing. Benjamin Franklin was a notable leader in promoting scientific study.

The fine arts movement was slowly beginning to emerge during the colonial period. No distinguished painters appeared until after 1760, although simple portraits had always remained quite popular. Classical music and theater arts grew in popularity and acceptance in the 1730s. Until the 1700s going to a play was considered sinful and plays were actually banned in most American colonies. While many considered theater to be immoral, growing sophistication and secular attitudes of the upper class inspired a desire to see live stage performances. Previously, Americans had only read the plays of the great masters, but most had never seen or acted in one.

EARLY NATIONAL PERIOD (1776–1840)

As we just read, during colonial times schooling was left up to each of the individual colonies. With the many different religions and ways of life, schooling was difficult to maintain and centralize. At the time of the American Revolution the school on the whole continued to occupy a relatively minor place in American life.

After 1776 the New England colonies focused on compulsory public education. They wanted all capable children to attend school and to be educated to become good citizens. The middle colonies' policies were that of parochial education. Schools were primarily for educating the children with powerful minds to become ministers, priests, clerks, or to hold government offices. The Southern colonies, on the other hand, didn't really have much in the line of compulsory education because of the ruralness of these areas. Most education in the South consisted of apprenticeships and the like.

In an effort to consolidate schools and make education mandatory, Congress enacted the Land Ordinance of 1785. This ordinance set aside what was known as Section Sixteen in every township in the new western territory for the maintenance of public schools. The separation of church and state was visible by now, and public schools were organized to corral the best minds for training for public leadership.

Two years later came the Northwest Ordinance of 1787. This ordinance provided land in the Great Lakes and Ohio Valley regions for settlement (Michigan, Indiana, Wisconsin, Ohio, and Illinois). Of particular interest is article 3 of the ordinance, which reads, in part, that religion, morality, and knowledge are necessary to good government and the happiness of mankind, and so schools and the means of education should forever be encouraged.

The Northwest Ordinance stated that education is necessary to become a good citizen and to have a strong government. Schools began to form everywhere. Teachers were subsidized to an extent by the government and the rest by state taxes. Schools began teaching more than just religion, reading, and spelling. Sciences were a part of the new curriculum.

New forms of education arose. New Harmony, Indiana, was established in 1825 as an experiment in cooperative living. Robert Owen, a British socialist, founded the community in order to provide a model town based on the principle of common ownership. All people were to be treated the same. Each member was to be given an equal education—boys as well as girls, and adults as well as young children. Owen believed that education should begin in early childhood, and New Harmony had one of the first infant schools in the United States.

The primary groups of people involved in this experiment were the industrial and agricultural working classes. The goal was to improve the lives of the working classes through education of the group. Classical, conventional education was eliminated and practical schooling that aimed to reform social, economic, and political conditions was chosen. Owen felt that children must feel secure before they could learn. He believed children should learn through their senses, not through lecturing. He would begin with "hands-on" experiences called the "object lessons" and gradually expand to the general concepts.

By 1827 the experiment in New Harmony had begun to fail because of disagreements between Owen and the community over education and finance. (Some things are timeless—much of our current dilemma regarding education still involves disagreement over finance and education.)

In 1828 Owen was forced to sell New Harmony at a loss. Although the experiment was short-lived the movement aroused public interest in education as a means to elevate and equalize social conditions.

Three prominent Americans highlighted the early national period. Benjamin Rush lived from 1746 to 1813 and was one of the leaders in the Revolutionary movement. He was a 1760 graduate of Princeton and also a graduate of Edinburgh in 1768. He was a professor at the College of Philadelphia when the Revolution broke out. He was interested in many social reforms with one of his top priorities being reform of American education. He wanted American education to be in line with American needs and work along with the principles of democracy.

In 1786, Rush produced a plan of education that he hoped would meet the needs of democracy. He believed, along with Adams, Madison, and others, that the only security of a republic lay in a proper education. Hence, Rush wrote the monumental essay entitled "Thoughts Upon the Mode of Education Proper in a Republic." This essay consisted of twenty main points, some of which are briefly summarized here:

- Education had to take place in the United States. A uniform system of education needed to be established that would make education in the United States preferred to an education in any other country.
- There was a supreme regard for their new country. The United States needed to establish a public system that would reinforce this rather than the motives that dominated private schools.

- It was preferable to devote to science the time then spent on the study of Greek and Latin. The prosperity and future development of the United States depended on the advancement of science and exploring its resources.
- The curriculum was to be suitable for American democracy.

Let the first eight years be employed in learning to speak, spell, read, and write the English language. Arithmetic and some of the more simple branches of mathematics should be acquired between the ages of twelve and fourteen. Natural history should find a prominent place early in the education process. Geography should be understood and mastered by age twelve and in place of the ancient languages should come French and German. Between the ages of fourteen and eighteen the student should be instructed in grammar, oratory, criticism, and higher branches of mathematics, philosophy, chemistry, logic, metaphysics, chronology, history, government, the principles of agriculture, manufacturing, and whatever else was needed for public usefulness and private happiness. (Butts and Cremin 1965)

It is interesting to note that Rush set up this curriculum for boys alone.

- Education, though limited, was required for females. Women had the responsibility of instructing their children and Rush felt that they should be prepared "by a suitable education, for the discharge of this most important duty as mothers." The woman had to be the manager of her home in order to carry out these various obligations. The main part of a woman's education should consist of a mastery of the English language and the ability to read and write well. The female curriculum consisted of knowledge of figures and bookkeeping, an acquaintance with geography, vocal music, dancing, the reading of history, travels, poetry, and moral essays. To these were added "regular instruction in the Christian religion." However, the purpose of a woman's education was for her to prepare the youth of her time to be guardians of democracy. It was not for her personal betterment.
- Schools were to teach forgetting. Rush was so convinced of the problems of copying European institutions that he suggested the need for the establishment of special schools to develop the skill of forgetting.
- Schools needed liberal national support for educated teachers. For any such system to go into effect, the nation should provide schools

and colleges adequately equipped with teachers well qualified for their task. The schools should be so liberally supported that all of the best talent should be attracted into the teaching profession.

The system of education that Rush advocated demanded training for both men and women for the understanding of the ways that democracy might be made effective, and for creating an atmosphere and attitude for the maintenance of democratic ideals.

When we think of Thomas Jefferson, we remember him as President Jefferson and think of the many great accomplishments he had while leading our young country. Some of his other accomplishments are just as important yet not as easily remembered. Such things that may fall into this category are his view and influence on the educational system and the importance of the right and freedom to an education.

Jefferson was born in 1743 and emerged as one of the greatest revolutionary leaders of our country. He was the primary author of the Declaration of Independence. His greatest accomplishment in the field of education took place after his political career ended. He spent the last years of his life creating the University of Virginia at Charlottesville. This school was a visionary new school introducing American youth to the new ideas about government and equality. He realized that different students have different academic needs and allowed for these differences by electives in his curriculum. He created the university as a place where both students and faculty would be able to enjoy the freedom and ability to learn. He also surveyed the site, planned the buildings, and supervised the construction. Thanks to his efforts and determination, the university opened in March of 1825.

Jefferson helped push education ahead and allowed for a strong foundation for future universities and colleges. Jefferson's will and drive were there to protect the "unlimitable freedom of the human mind to explore and to expose every subject susceptible of its contemplation" (Barger 2000). If it were not for Jefferson, the educational system as we know it might not exist today.

Benjamin Franklin (1706–1790) was an American printer, author, diplomat, philosopher, and scientist whose many contributions to the American Revolution—and the newly formed federal government that followed—ranked him among the country's greatest statesmen.

Franklin believed that science could solve the problems of human life and that knowledge came from the senses—observations and experimentation. He believed that knowledge should be applied to human affairs, the economy, and society. He valued formal education and schooling and he established a plan for an English language grammar school in Philadelphia in 1749. The proposal was important because it exposed the stimulus for a new education to accompany the new republic.

The school would teach English rather than Latin, and devise a curriculum that illustrated scientific and practical skills. It would provide knowledge that would prepare people who could make contributions to society, politics, government, and to occupations and professions. He wanted the school equipped with laboratories and workshops that contained books, maps, globes, and so forth, so that students would be aware of the relationships between learning and the environment around them. The teachers would emphasize both practical and ethical elements of the skills and subjects that they taught.

The English grammar school did not flourish. The headmaster did not want to implement the innovations required for the school's success. His management style was rigid in the traditional focus on Latin and Greek. Franklin's educational proposals illustrated the emergent trends of the Revolutionary and early national periods and also anticipated the course of America's future in education. The scientific and utilitarian subjects and methods broke sharply with the classical tradition. This showed the En-glish language would become the language of educated persons involved in building a new nation. His proposals pointed the way to a more comprehensive educational institution that would offer students a varied curriculum suited to the needs of an emerging and developing nation.

COMMON SCHOOL PERIOD (1840–1880)

This period brought us the kindergarten, a classroom program consisting of children ages three to seven years of age. The programs range from half days to full days depending on the school system.

There was a kindergarten in Watertown, Wisconsin, founded by Margarethe Schurz in 1856. Elizabeth Peabody established one in Boston in 1873. The original idea was that children need to have playtime in order to learn. Kindergarten should be a place for children to grow and learn from their social interaction with other children. Through systematic play the children are able to learn to discriminate, analyze, share, and solve problems. Kindergarten programs were also established to help children of poverty and those who had special needs.

On July 3, 1839, three young women reported to Lexington, Massachusetts, with hopes of attending the first state-funded school specifically established for public teacher education (what was then referred to as a "normal" school). After taking an examination that determined they were satisfactorily versed in the subjects taught by the ordinary district school, they were granted admission to this experimental program, the first in the nation.

For the upper classes there existed some good colleges providing a classical education for ministry, law, or medicine. Teacher education was not considered a profession worthy of their attention. Public schools at this point were in bad shape. Typically in session for only four months of the year (because of the agrarian society and the need to have children helping out at home), they were poorly attended and basically taught by whomever was available. The pay of thirty dollars per month was not much of a motivation for potential teachers to seek out an education specific to the occupation or for existing colleges to provide it to their employees.

However, the direction of education was being influenced by the teaching methods of Prussian schools (directing the child in the unfolding of his latent powers and development of the individual's faculties into a complete personality). This was a far cry from rote memorization used in America's schools. Fostering critical thinking became the focus.

The spread of normal schools can in part be credited to twenty-six graduates of the third Massachusetts normal school opened in Bridgewater in 1840. These graduates went on to become normal school head managers as far away as Illinois and Michigan.

The normal schools attempted to provide the prospective teacher with a laboratory for learning, using model classrooms as a place to practice their new skills. The emphasis was on common everyday learning. The normal school crusade advocated teaching as a profession.

Compulsory education came about during the common school period. The Compulsory Attendance Act of 1852 enacted by the state of Massachusetts was the first general law attempting to control the conditions of children. The law included mandatory attendance for children between the ages of eight and fourteen for at least three months out of each year; of these twelve weeks at least six had to be consecutive. Exceptions to this law included proof that the child had already learned the subjects, poverty, or the physical or mental inability of the child to attend.

In 1873 the Compulsory Attendance Law was revised. The age limit was reduced to twelve but the annual attendance was increased to twenty weeks per year.

Since the first law in 1852, the goals of education remain the same and have been gradually improving the conditions of children by supporting the restrictions on child labor. Compulsory education laws and child labor laws have worked hand in hand to advance the rights of children.

The Kalamazoo case of 1875 was brought about by a lawsuit filed to collect public funds for the support of a village high school. The town had used taxes to support the school for thirteen years without complaints from the citizens. The defendants in the case—the school officials—felt that a select few out of thousands need not dispute their obligation to pay taxes for the purpose of supporting a high school. The school officials supported their case with many previous court cases that upheld their position of financial support. The townships were required by state law to maintain the schools under threat of a large penalty for noncompliance. The Kalamazoo case used this law to establish the precedent of tax-supported schools with curriculums that included reading, writing, arithmetic, orthography, and decent behavior. Other territories followed suit.

New industrialization offered many opportunities in the United States. Great numbers of people recognized the possibilities and prepared to take advantage of them. From 1830 to 1850 more than one million Catholic immigrants came to the eastern seaboard of the United States and settled in the large urban areas where work was abundant and housing available. These Catholic immigrants were embarking on a new life in a strange land controlled by Protestants. This difference in religious belief resulted in prejudice and discrimination against Catholics who were the minority. This discrimination eventually led to the Catholic school system.

THE CATHOLIC ISSUE

Religion was a focal point of education in this period and the Protestants were in control. The public schools used the King James translation of the Bible, which the Catholics strongly objected to. Catholics did not accept the teachings of the Protestant Church or schools as they were then constituted. The Catholic Church tells her children that they must be taught the religion by authority. The Protestants say read the Bible and judge for yourselves. Catholic parents believed that the education of their children would be most beneficial with the use of Catholic Bibles and prayers. This request was denied. Catholic children were forced to become more Protestant if they were to be educated. Therefore, the development of a parochial school system became an absolute necessity. However, setting up the schools presented a problem: money.

Governor William H. Seward of New York was willing to use public funds to aid parochial schools but the common council, supported by the Protestant churches, rejected the idea. Bishop Francis Kenrick asked if Catholic children might be permitted to read from the Douay Bible instead of the King James Bible. The school board agreed to this offer, but Protestant religious newspapers and speakers were vocal about their disagreement. As a result discrimination against Catholics escalated. Riots, burning of Catholic churches, and several deaths occurred.

The denial of Catholics' request to use their own bible and prayers in the public schools left no other alternative but to establish a parochial school system in order to keep unity in the church. This led to many denials for funding and escalated to more violence. In fact, the more effective the Catholic offensive became, the more violent the Protestant opposition. The Catholic system was unable to design and have accepted a curriculum impregnated throughout with Catholic religious teaching. The Catholics feared a loss of support for their church if Catholic children were to attend public school. Opposition by Protestants continued and discrimination against Catholics mounted. Finally, a legal case (*Donahoe v. Richards*) led to further uproar. The Supreme Court of Maine decided that a school board had the legal and constitutional right to expel a child from school for refusing to read the Bible used by the school. The results of the controversy of the 1840s gave Catholics the final impetus to build their parochial school system that still exists today.

FATHER OF AMERICAN EDUCATION

The common school period brought us the "Father of American Education," Horace Mann, who was born in Franklin, Massachusetts, in 1796. Mann's schooling consisted of brief and erratic periods of eight to ten weeks a year. He educated himself by reading ponderous volumes from the Franklin Town Library. This self-education, combined with the fruits of a brief period of study with an itinerant schoolmaster, was sufficient to gain him admission to the sophomore class of Brown University in 1816. He went on to study law and finally received admission to the bar in 1823. Mann won a seat in the state legislature and in 1833 won a state senate seat (Cremin 1957).

Of the many causes dear to Mann's heart, none was closer than the education of the people. He held a keen interest in school policy and in 1837 left his law practice and accepted the post of the newly founded secretary of education. During his years in that post, Mann published twelve annual reports on the integral relationship between education, freedom, and the republican government. He advocated for a school that would be available and equal for all, part of the birth right of every American child. Social harmony was the primary goal of the school.

Mann felt that a common school would be the "great equalizer." Poverty would most assuredly disappear as a broadened popular intelligence tapped new treasures of natural and material wealth. He felt that through education crime would decline sharply as would moral vices like violence and fraud.

What is most important about Mann's view of the common school is that he saw in it an educational purpose truly common to all. As secretary of education, Mann presided over the establishment of the first public normal school in the United States. He also reinvigorated the 1827 law establishing high schools, and fifty high schools were created during his tenure. Mann also persuaded the Massachusetts legislature to establish a six-month minimum school year in 1839. In 1848 Mann resigned as secretary of education and went on to the United States House of Representatives, and then took the post of president of Antioch College. He stayed at the college until his death in 1859. Mann ultimately won his victory for humanity, as the public school became one of the characteristic features of American life.

PROGRESSIVE PERIOD (1880–1920)

Business and industry had a strong impact on American education. During the progressive period American business and industry rapidly expanded and there was also an increase in the number of immigrants entering the United States. Friedrich Taylor helped this expansion with the "efficiency movement." This movement was concerned with making the factories more efficient in producing more with less cost, effort, and material.

The schools were influenced by this efficiency movement. The school was viewed as a workplace and learning was perceived in terms of productivity. The schools were like factories, with the teachers as factory workers and the students as raw material to be turned into the product that was to meet the specifications of the needs of the twentieth century. In roughly half a century a vigorous, young agricultural people healed the wounds of a disastrous Civil War and became a leading industrial world power.

The public schools' mission was to assimilate the new immigrants into a nation that would remain English speaking and thinking. The children who could not be processed to completion were considered "scraps" to be dropped out of the production line, which is where we get our most accurate definition of "drop outs."

Due to the large size of the immigrant families most parents wanted to send their children into the workforce instead of school. These families wanted to benefit from the income they would receive if more of the family worked. This led to the compulsory attendance and child labor laws. These laws were mandated by each individual state to ensure that the immigrant children were in school receiving an education and not working in industry.

Schools now were concerned with deportment, diet, hygiene, and cleanliness. They were also a social mechanism for changing the behaviors of immigrant children who were, like their parents, rudely transported from farm villages to the ghettos and crowded areas of America's larger cities.

The progressive period brought about the development of the role of the principal. The principal serves as a sort of middle person, a liaison between central administration and the teachers. The educational field was not always organized this way. Originally, students were taught in single-room schools with every age group, ability level, and subject taught by one teacher. As population increased and the schools started to provide more services it was clear that there was a need for more teachers to help carry out the teaching and clerical duties.

The original principal was actually called a principal teacher. The principal teacher fulfilled many roles in the community (teacher, town clerk, grave digger, church chorister, court messenger, and sometimes even the church bell ringer). The concept of a principal teacher started at the high school level and eventually caught on at the primary level of education. Eventually, the teaching and other duties that were required became too time consuming, and principal teachers then concentrated on managing the schools (this is when they dropped the "teacher" in their role as principal teacher). Today the role focuses on leadership and the managing of the school as well as serving as a liaison between the teachers and central administration.

Educational administration was brought about in this period following the development of principal teachers. Educational administration was too important to be left to teachers to manage. The public felt that leadership needed to be centralized. Trends in education can be linked to those of society. A good example of this is at the turn of the century when the main goal of education was to prepare European immigrants to assume jobs in our booming industry. This drew attention to the field of administration. New York, under French influence, was the first state really to concern itself with the development of centralized school organization and the first state to create the office of superintendent. The term "superintendent of schools" grew out of the terminology of the times (superintendent of the railroad, industrial plant superintendent, etc.).

The progressive period introduced the concept of dividing the school into grades. In the early days of this country, education was usually left for the elite. This was accomplished by individual attention in the forms of tutoring and small single-room schools. After the Revolutionary War, Congress enacted several bills to encourage education for all children.

These single-room schools usually housed thirty to forty students of all ages and levels with one teacher. In some districts, the teacher would even stay at each of the children's homes for a few weeks in return for their teaching. In some of the larger single-room schools, the teacher would instruct the older, more experienced students, who in turn would teach the younger and lower-level students.

As more and more children were attending school, the single-room schools could no longer handle the demand for education that all of the children needed at so many different levels and ages. The government and the separate states were beginning to draw up requirements for education. The easiest way to overcome the crowded and run-down buildings was to construct new buildings with many different classrooms. Students began coming in to the schools from surrounding communities and this added to the need for larger buildings.

Guidelines for teachers became evident, also. Teachers had training to teach certain subjects and levels. But one question remained: What was the best way to split up the children with respect to their levels and needs? The best answer they found was age. At different ages, the students had different needs and the best way to meet these needs was to group every-one in the same age brackets together. Initially, many of the small schools grouped together with several ages in one room. Grades one, two, and three would be together, while grades four, five, and six were in another area. Then came grades seven and eight. If students moved on past these levels, they would usually attend colleges or universities.

As the populations grew and expanded westward, the need for larger district schools became clear. The grades were separated into their own levels, and mandates were set for what had to be taught at each grade. The rise of elementary and secondary schools came about. Today we operate on a twelve-grade system, plus kindergarten. It is amazing to see how schools have grown from single-room buildings to large corporations with many schools to accommodate the youth of America.

THE RISE OF THE HIGH SCHOOL

Education has not always been an ingrained part of the American lifestyle. When America was first being settled, the colonists brought with them the form of education used in their homeland. This mixture of systems eventually melded together into the American educational system. The simple harsh realities of life, however, made education a luxury instead of a priority during these early years. For a long time the majority of schooling was accomplished by teaching the basics of reading, writing, arithmetic, and religion. Since school attendance was not required due to conditions of rural life in the colonies, only about one out of every ten children actually went to school. Many children either helped their parents scratch out a living or went into apprenticeship with a local tradesman. For those rich enough to afford the luxury, tutors were hired or the children were sent away to tuition schools in England.

One of the major problems was actually finding schoolmasters for the schools. Teaching was not a respected position in any community. It was difficult to maintain any type of living on the salaries that they were earning. Pay was often received in the form of a cow, a pig, a bushel of apples, or a load of firewood.

With such teaching conditions, those who chose to work in the schools were not of the best temperament. Many of the students received more discipline than lessons from schoolmasters, who were chosen for their size and manner as opposed to their scholastic credentials. The older boys would make a sport of running the schoolmaster out of town, so only the strong could handle the job.

The development of the high school received a boost from Benjamin Franklin in 1751 when a new type of secondary education, the academy, was formed. It focused on subjects that could be directly related to the students' adult lives. Another leap was made in allowing girls to attend. Primarily girls were allowed to attend more primitive forms of elementary education when they were young, but then they were expected to stay at home and learn domestic skills until they could be suitably married off.

The first true publicly supported high school was formed in 1824. As the number of schools grew, so did the quality of education. Classes such as algebra, American history, bookkeeping, geometry, and surveying were quickly added to the sparse curriculum. Three hundred high schools were added by the time of the Civil War. By 1880 there were eight hundred high schools in the United States and by 1890 there were 2500.

Even the purpose of the high school has changed. Their main intention went from preparing students for college to preparing students for life and nonacademic jobs. High school diplomas suddenly became tickets into good colleges and students began to see the real value of higher education and the impact it could have on their lives. Change and adaptability were the mottos of the education community and this new surge of interest in public education paved the way for the educational system as we know it today.

Changes were needed because of increased enrollment in secondary schools. A new focus that would take into account individual differences, goals, attitudes, and abilities was adopted. This led to the seven cardinal principles of secondary education, started in 1915 and finished in 1918. They were issued by the Commission on the Reorganization of Secondary Education. The seven cardinal principles are:

- Command of fundamental processes (writing, reading, oral and written expression, and mathematics)
- Health
- Worthy home membership (This principle "calls for the development of those qualities that make the individual a worthy member of a family, both contributing to and deriving benefit from that membership" [Raubinge et al. 1969, 108].)
- Vocation (the student gets to know him or herself and a variety of careers so that the student can choose the most suitable career.)
- Civic education (develop an awareness and concern of one's own community)
- Worthy use of leisure (Education should give the student the skills to enrich his/her body, mind, spirit, and personality in his/her leisure.)
- Ethical character (instilling in the student the notion of personal responsibility and initiative)

Finally, the progressive period brought the manual training movement, which was the precursor to the vocational training program in our schools today. First used in the United States in the 1870s in the training of engineers, the movement spread rapidly to general public education.

Manual training emphasized the intellectual and social development associated with the practical training of the hand and the eye. In its most basic sense, manual training was the teaching of both wood and metal working, with the accompanying argument that this teaching improved perception, observation, practical judgment, visual accuracy, manual dexterity, and taught students the power of doing things instead of merely thinking about them, talking about them, and writing about them. School directors emphasized that manual training was not intended to teach a specific trade. This was perceived as too narrow and intellectually limiting for a general education. Manual training would be an enhancement to the traditional curriculum, not a replacement, and would help achieve the full development of potential of the individual. The student would learn to skillfully use tools in drafting, mechanics, woodworking, or metalworking, and then would be able to transfer this knowledge to almost any kind of tool or setting. Leaders of industry and statesmen turned to the schools to develop training programs to replace and supplement the apprenticeship system.

The trend of the times stated that a sound education needed to include both vocational and general education. An example of this was the Manual Training School for boys, which opened in 1879 in St. Louis, Missouri. The curriculum included science, mathematics, language, literature, history, drawing, and shop work. Shop was included to keep instruction more interesting, to provide learning in the use of basic tools common to a variety of jobs, and to increase general education. Educators felt that manual training was essential for proper intellectual and moral education and was also a way of restoring the value and dignity of hand labor. Manual training would help students realize at an early age the connection between knowing and doing. "The contrast between the listless and often inattentive attitude of children occupied with some ordinary class lesson, and the eager eyes and nimble fingers of the same children at the carpenter's bench or modeling bench, is most instructive," wrote Sir Philip Magnus, one of the early supporters of manual training (Woodward 1969, 87).

Critics of the manual training movement argued that manual training did not belong in the schools, and, if introduced, would hinder students' intellectual and moral development. Debate continued with proponents recognizing the potential for intellectual development though the training of the hand and the eye as well as the potential for occupational payoff. This would then benefit the overall economy of the region.

By 1900, one hundred cities provided manual training in their high schools. In the years following, manual training became more subject centered, required the completion of specific exercises, and was oriented to skill development. Vocational education in secondary schools had become an accepted part of American education.

MODERN PERIOD (1920–PRESENT)

Three prominent men highlight the early years of the modern period. G. Stanley Hall fathered the testing movement. He was born in Ashfield,

Massachusetts, in 1844, and was an educator and an American psychologist in the field of adolescence. He focused his attention on the educational needs of adolescents.

From 1889 to 1920, the high school focus was primarily college preparatory, emphasizing Latin, modern foreign languages, mathematics, science, English, and history. However, Hall objected strongly to the college preparatory view, arguing that high school should be more concerned with the education of adolescents. He founded the *American Journal of Psychology* in 1887 and under his guidance considerable work was done in educational research.

Scientific research in child development flourished. One major stimulus was the introduction of the Stanford–Benet intelligence test. This test led to a number of studies about children's intellectual development. Hall went on to conclude that each stage of a child's development, while distinct and unique, was related to the totality of human development. For each stage, there was appropriate learning and activities. Hall said that the curriculum should come from the child and be based on his or her interests and needs.

John Dewey, often called the father of modern education, simply stated that education and communication is the necessity of teaching and learning for the continued existence of a society. Dewey said that there is more than a verbal tie between the words common, community, and communication. What we must have in common in order to form a community or society are aims, beliefs, aspirations, knowledge—a common understanding (Dewey 1916).

Dewey felt that at that time the relations of parent and child, teacher and pupil, and employer and employee did not form a true social group. Giving and taking of orders modifies action and results, but does not of itself effect a sharing of purposes, a communication of interests.

Education is crucial to social life. This education insists in transmission through communication. Dewey relayed that communication is a process of sharing experiences until it becomes a common possession. As societies become more complex in structure and resources, the need of formal or intentional teaching and learning increases. As formal teaching and training grow in extent there is danger of creating an undesirable split between the experience gained in more direct associations and what is acquired in school. This is a danger ever present whenever there is a rapid growth of knowledge and technical modes of skill.

George Counts (1889–1974) was a prominent educational sociologist. He believed in the child-centered movement in progressive education. He wanted teachers to lead society instead of following society. The teachers were leaders and should be policymakers who could decide between conflicting purposes and values. Teachers should be concerned with school issues, but should also be concerned with controversial issues of economics, politics, and morality. Counts believed the school was an agency involved in society's politics, economics, art, religion, and ethics (Ornstein and Levine 1993, 144). If the school was involved it could either reflect the knowledge, beliefs, and values of society or it could seek to change them. The schools had to help solve problems. Schools needed to identify with such progressive forces as labor unions, farmers' organizations, and minority groups. By joining with groups that wanted to change society, the schools could then make social improvements. Counts believed teachers could help change society.

The year is now 1950. While other children were running, playing, and doing their homework, one little girl was simply trying to get an education. When Linda Carol Brown was seven years old, she became the center of a major court battle that would set a precedent for segregation laws everywhere. Linda was required to attend Monroe School in East Topeka, Kansas, because it was one of the four all-black schools in the city. Linda's father tried unsuccessfully to enroll her in the third grade at an all-white public school. He then teamed up with the National Association for the Advancement of Colored People (NAACP) to fight her unfair exclusion. The Kansas lawsuit, along with similar lawsuits from Delaware, South Carolina, and Virginia, were all compiled under the legal case *Brown v. Board of Education*. The momentous decision that was made two years later is still viewed as one of the most important and significant rulings that the Supreme Court has made in the last century.

The main issue that was focused on in this case was whether or not the Fourteenth Amendment was violated by denying education in a specific school simply due to race. The Fourteenth Amendment states, in summary, that no person who is a citizen of the United States should be denied equal protection under the law or the right to life, liberty, or property. What had to be decided was if segregation fell under the idea of equal protection. This was a major issue because seventeen states were still segregating their schools, four states gave the option of segregation to school districts, eleven states had no laws regarding segregation, and sixteen states flatly prohibited it.

By May 17, 1954, four years after Linda Brown's rejection from the school in Topeka, Kansas, the Supreme Court had reached a unanimous decision. Segregation was in violation of the law. Although the case of *Brown v. Board of Education* has not solved all of the racial problems in this country, it was a major step in the right direction.

The modern period brought help to those citizens who needed extra money for education. Thanks to the G.I. Bill, the National Defense Education Act (NDEA), and the Elementary and Secondary Education Act (ESEA) Americans were able to reach higher education.

The Elementary and Secondary Education Act of 1965 was a federal response to the social change taking place in American society. Many African-American students as well as members of other minority groups, especially in inner-city areas, were educationally disadvantaged because of social and economic conditions. The ESEA encouraged special programs for children of low-income families and this related to President Lyndon Johnson's War on Poverty, which also encouraged special programs for economically and culturally disadvantaged children. Title I was an offshoot of this program, helping children gain up to a year or more in mathematics and reading achievement.

In the years between 1965 and 1980 things were relatively calm. Then in 1983 a report was published that made it imperative for educational reform. *A Nation at Risk* was a report that was issued by the National Commission on Excellence in Education. Secondary curricula were closely examined and it was found that the curricula no longer had a central purpose unifying all of the subjects.

The state of American education was deemed terrible. Many countries in the world were matching and surpassing our educational attainments. Twenty-three million American adults were functionally illiterate by the simplest test of everyday reading, writing, and comprehension. Thirteen percent of all seventeen-year-olds in the United States could not read or write. Compared to other nations, American youth spent much less time on schoolwork. Economic repercussions were presumed to occur because of this poor state of American education. We were losing our competitive edge in the world's economic market. These findings were considered depressing when one took into account the high demand for skilled workers in scientific and technological fields.

The report recommended five new basics to be added to the curriculum in American schools. These basics included four years of English, three years of mathematics, three years of science, three years of social studies, and half a year of computer science.

Specific standards were established as to what should be accomplished by these five basics. In English, high school graduates should be able to:

- Comprehend, interpret, evaluate, and use what they read.
- Write well-organized, effective papers.
- Listen effectively and discuss ideas intelligently.
- Know our literary heritage and how it relates to the customs, ideas, and values of today's life and culture.

In mathematics, high school graduates should be able to:

- Understand algebraic and geometric concepts.
- Understand elementary probability and statistics.
- Apply math in everyday situations.
- Estimate, approximate, measure, and test for accuracy of the calculations.

As a way to increase our educational position in the world it was recommended that teaching, teacher education, and educational standards be reformed. The virtues of lifelong learning were also extolled.

Students' rights became an issue. Educators were convinced that student rights do not end at the schoolhouse gate. Administrators could not make decisions about student suspensions if they violated the Fourteenth Amendment right to due process of law—students had the right to notice and some kind of hearing when involved in rule violation, which was not happening. Students also had the right to freedom of speech and expression as stated in the First Amendment. Two landmark cases involving students' rights are the *Tinker v. Des Moines* and *Goss v. Lopez* cases. Both cases were won by the students and the students' rights foundation was set.

One of the most important pieces of legislation passed in the twentieth century was Public Law 94-142. This law was intended to improve opportunities in education for handicapped children and adults through the provision of a free and appropriate public education in the "least restrictive environment." This legislation mandates that handicapped students be educated with children and adults who are not handicapped, and that special classes, separate schools, or other removal of children from their regular educational environment occurs only when the severity of the handicap is such that education in regular classes cannot be achieved.

A huge piece of our educational history includes charter schools, magnet schools, and home schooling. Charter schools have emerged as one of the most popular approaches to reform. Charters are truly flexible, self-defining alternatives for public school reform. The possibilities for innovation, as a vehicle to think differently and organize in new ways, are strong. Charters provide choice for both teachers and students.

The charter movement makes for strange bedfellows. Federal, state, and local policymakers have jumped on the charter school bandwagon in part because its proponents come from diverse constituencies including Republicans, Democrats, teacher organizations, business groups, and parent associations. The uniting forces are a general concern with the academic performance of people in district public schools and a belief that charter schools can improve the situation.

A charter school is an independent public school of choice, given a charter or contract for a specified period of time (three to five years) to educate children according to the school's own design, with a minimum of bureaucratic oversight. It may be a new school, started from scratch, or an existing one that secedes from its school district. It is held accountable to the terms of the charter and continues to exist only if it fulfills those terms. As a public school of choice, it is attended by students whose families select it and staffed by educators who choose to teach in it.

Charters bring conversations about the proper role, scope, and purpose of public education out of the offices of policy wonks and into the kitchens of parents to discuss what type of school their children should attend. Charters bring policy making out of state legislatures and into neighborhood centers where community members debate the appropriateness of a particular charter school for their city or town. Charters bring professional discussions about how best to teach children out of the administrative buildings of school districts and into the school hallways as teachers think about where their talents and energies would be best devoted and sometimes choose to bring their dreams to life in a school of their own.

Chances of success improve when the charter school has strong leadership, when there is a clear and focused vision, and when interested parties work together as a team exceptionally well. Charter schools pride themselves on their independence and flexibility, but they are still publicly funded schools accountable to taxpayers. The level of accountability found in charter schools should be built into all of our public schools.

To many educators, parents, and politicians, the charter school idea represented a public education alternative. It was an idea they could embrace enthusiastically because it seemed to protect public education as an institution and at the same time provide for fundamental reform and systematic restructuring. As a bonus, charter schools have more media sex appeal than site-based management.

In 1991, Minnesota became the first state to pass a charter school law. The Minnesota legislation enabled school districts to "charter" schools organized by teachers and parents. These schools were freed of most state and local regulations and operated as nonprofit corporations that were legally autonomous.

Charter schools provide the local control with accountability that many educators support and thousands of parents and community members want. They provide an infusion of inspiration and energy from within the public school system itself.

The goal of the charter school movement is not just to establish innovative schools but also to help improve the public education system. They are challenging traditional forms of public education. Joe Nathan, director of the Center for School Change, says that charter schools are an especially good option because they promise two-way accountability. They declare what they will do for students and then must provide solid evidence to families and taxpayers that they are doing what they promised. Nathan says that schools exist in part to serve the needs of society so it is entirely appropriate for the public to set expectations for any instruction that receives public funds (Nathan 1996).

In the face of great challenges to our urban school systems, many other reformers believe that schools with specially defined missions, such as magnet schools, offer better academic opportunities to urban youth. In recent years magnet schools—schools with specially focused missions—have proliferated in urban areas. Magnet schools are needed to help overcome the family and community breakdown often found in urban areas. Students feel isolated and lost in the throws of poverty and crime and need alternatives. As students engage in a common mission they may form strong social ties. These social ties lead to academic success as students renew an interest in a special focus they feel is designed especially for their needs.

When families choose a magnet school, they are asserting an interest in the school's particular mission, and it links them with other families and teachers who have presumably chosen the school for similar reasons. Students appear to form social relationships around the magnet school's specialized aims, leading to better academic experiences.

Finally, home schooling has become an important resource for studying how children learn. Families are more interested in what is best for the individualized learner. Home schools take into account personality differences and stages, not ages, and the method is enjoying increased popularity. On any given day more than a half million children are home schooled (Lines 1996).

As we round out our history on American education, we note that in late 1989, then president George H. W. Bush and the nation's governors met in Virginia for a bipartisan "education summit." At this summit, the groundwork was laid for the national education goals, which were all part of the Goals 2000 Educational Program. Under the Bush administration, the program was called "America 2000."

The goals were not to be used for political gain nor as a hollow promise. They were the centerpiece for educational reform in both the Bush and the Clinton administrations. They serve as a nationwide pact by which we can measure the output of our educational systems throughout America.

The passing of the Goals 2000: Educate America Act on March 31, 1994, allowed the federal government a new role in its support for education. The federal government can now promote a comprehensive approach to help all students succeed in life.

These goals are listed below, followed by current information about why these goals are needed. By the year 2000:

1. Every child will start school ready to learn.
2. The high school graduation rate will increase to at least 90 percent.

3. American students will leave grades four, eight, and twelve having demonstrated competency over challenging subject matter including English, mathematics, science, foreign language, social studies, and art. Every school in America will insure that all students learn to use their knowledge in order to be prepared for responsible citizenship, further learning, and productive employment in our modern economy.
4. The teaching force will have access to programs for the continued improvement of their professional skills.
5. America's students will be first in the world in science and mathematics.
6. Every adult American will be literate and will posses the knowledge and skills necessary to compete in a global economy.
7. Every school in the United States will be free of drugs, alcohol, violence, and weapons.
8. Every school will promote partnerships that will increase parental involvement and participation in promoting the social, emotional, and academic growth of children.

Educators believe that these goals are needed for many (Barger 2000):

The first goal is needed because almost half of American babies start life behind and never have the support to catch up, 45 percent are born with risk factors for further learning and development, and only 37 percent are immunized against major childhood diseases by age two. Just over half (53 percent) of our preschool children are read to daily and less than half (43 percent) are aware of family history or ethnic heritage.

Goal two is needed because only 78 percent of our teenagers complete high school.

Goals three and five are necessary because fewer than one-in-five fourth and twelfth graders, and one-in-four eight graders, understand complex mathematical theory; similar figures have been found in measurement of reading ability.

Goal six is important because many Americans have only basic literacy— only 52 percent of the population can perform challenging literacy tasks in reading and mathematics.

Goal seven is needed because only 50 percent of our high school students feel safe at school, 53 percent believe that other's misbehaviors interfere with their learning, and 28 percent have been offered drugs in school.

People are divided in their support of Goals 2000. Many feel this will lead to a federal government takeover of local education. They fear a federal government mandate, direction, or control over a state, local education agency, or school's curriculum. Others believe Goals 2000 will encourage local school systems into meeting educational needs, help students reach their potential, increase parent involvement, and improve teacher skills. Time will tell if Goals 2000 will help rebuild our educational system.

Creating different school programs and offering parents choices among them makes sense because there is no "one best school" for every child. We are witnessing an explosion of interest in creating new types of schools and giving parents the power to choose among them. In the past twenty-five years support has built for increasing the variety of options within public education and for giving parents more power to decide which options suit their child best. Advocates say that greater variety among schools will increase the likelihood that parents will find a school that matches their educational values and their child's learning needs.

As a manager, you must create a school that *stands* for something substantively or pedagogically or both, and then give people an incentive to attend. This allows both parents and teachers to commit to a common mission or focus of a school, rather than being assigned for strictly bureaucratic reasons. For many parents, the social, racial, and ethnic characteristics of a school's students are more important than a school's curriculum or its academic effectiveness.

Criticism of the educational system throughout history has stemmed from differences of value and interest. Six issues have remained of concern since the United States was born: religion, discipline, academics, vocation, individual needs, and society's demands. Curriculum makers at all levels of the educational system were torn by them. If one was responded to, criticism arose from proponents of the others. Experts are still struggling.

The history of education, therefore, should be designed to help educators understand what their problems are, how the problems have arisen, what the advantages and dangers of the past have been, what forces from the past are still at work in the present, and what we have to reckon with as we move into the future.

Historically, education in the United States was designed to meet the needs of religious, agricultural, and industrial powers; yet, in today's

America, learning is based on a student becoming a successful person in any field he or she chooses. Women were also greatly ignored in regards to higher education throughout America's history, which has completely changed in modern society. From a sociological perspective, schools had to change to meet the needs of modern Americans.

Efforts to improve education in America will in all likelihood continue throughout the new millennium. In the past, many of these reform efforts have been thwarted by myths and misinformation that propel opposition to enhancements in systems and methods of educating America's youth. As the nation continues to debate the issues of education, and continues to plan programs of reform, it is important to remember that these movements are far more effective when they are based on knowledge derived from researching education's function in society over time. What we have done in the past shapes our present and impacts our future.

2

Managing versus Leading

You must see the change you wish to see.

—Mahatma Gandhi

Are you a manager or a leader? Although you may hear these two terms thrown out interchangeably, they are two very different animals complete with different personalities and worldviews.

Let us take a look at the different personality styles of managers and leaders, the attitudes each have toward their goals, their basic conceptions of what their work entails, their relationships with others, and their sense of self (or self-identity) and how it develops. It is necessary also to examine leadership development and discover what criteria is necessary for leaders and managers to reach their full potential in our schools.

Let's start with definitions dealing with management. *The Random House Dictionary of English Language* gives the following definitions:

Manage: To bring about or succeed in accomplishing, sometimes despite difficulty or hardship; to take charge or care of; to dominate or influence by tact, flattery, or artifice; to handle, direct, govern, or control in action or use.

Management: The act or manner of managing, direction, handling, or control; persons or person controlling and directing the affairs of a business or institution.

Manager: The person who has control or direction of an institution, business, etc. or of a part, division, or phase of it. A person who controls and manipulates resources and expenditures.

Merriam-Webster's Third New International Dictionary contains these definitions:

Manage: Control and direct, handle either with or will cope with, guide by careful or delicate treatment; to bring about by contriving; succeed in doing or accomplishing to achieve one's purpose.

Management: More or less skilled handing of something conducting or supervision of; planning, organizing, supervising any activity with responsibility for results.

PERSONALITY DIFFERENCES

There are significant differences in personality styles between managers and leaders. Managers emphasize rationality and control, are problem solvers (focusing on goals, resources, organizational structures, or people), persistent, tough minded, hard working, intelligent, analytical, and tolerant. Managers often ask, "What problems have to be solved, and what are the best ways to achieve results?"

Leaders can visualize a purpose and generate value in work, are imaginative, passionate, nonconforming, risk takers, and often need to achieve control of themselves before they try to control others.

Managers and leaders have very different attitudes toward goals. Managers adopt impersonal, almost passive attitudes toward goals, decide upon goals based on necessity instead of desire (and are therefore deeply tied to their organization's culture), and tend to be reactive since they focus on current information.

Leaders tend to be active since they envision and promote their ideas instead of reacting to current situations, shape ideas instead of responding to them, have a personal orientation toward goals, and provide a vision that alters the way people think about what is desirable, possible, and necessary.

DIFFERENCES IN CONCEPTION OF WORK

Managers view work as an enabling process, establishing strategies and making decisions by combining people and ideas. They continually coordinate and balance opposing views, are good at reaching compromises and mediating conflicts between opposing values and perspectives and act to limit choice.

Leaders develop new approaches to long-standing problems and open issues to new options, use their vision to excite people, focus people on shared ideas and raise their expectations, and work from high-risk positions because of strong dislike of mundane work.

RELATIONSHIP DIFFERENCES

Managers prefer working with others, are collaborative, maintain a low level of emotional involvement in relationships, attempt to reconcile differences, seek compromises and establish a balance of power, focus on how things get done, maintain controlled rational and equitable structures, and may be viewed by others as inscrutable, detached, and manipulative.

Leaders maintain inner perceptiveness that they can use in their relationships with others, relate to people in intuitive, empathetic ways, focus on what it means to participate in events and decisions, create systems where human relations may be turbulent, intense, and at times even disorganized.

DIFFERENCES IN SELF-IDENTITY

Managers report that their adjustments to life have been straight forward and that their lives have been more or less peaceful since birth; have a sense of self as a guide to conduct behavior and attitude, which is derived from a feeling of being at home and in harmony with their environment; see themselves as conservators and regulators of an existing order of affairs with which they personally identify and from which they gain rewards and perpetuate and strengthen existing institutions; and display a lifelong development process that focuses on socialization. This socialization process prepares managers to guide schools and to maintain the existing balance of social relations.

Leaders reportedly have not had an easy time of it; their lives are marked by a continual struggle to find some sense of order, and they do not take things for granted and are not satisfied with the status quo. Leaders report that their "sense of self" is derived from a feeling of profound separateness. They may work in schools, but never have the feeling that a school "belongs" to them. (Principals seldom stay in a school more than five years.) Leaders seek opportunities for change (technological, political, or ideological), support change, and find their purpose is to profoundly alter human, economic, and political relationships.

Bennis (1999, 9) defines the differences between managers and leaders as follows:

- The manager administers; the leader innovates.
- The manager maintains; the leader develops.
- The manager accepts reality; the leader investigates it.
- The manager focuses on systems and structures; the leader focuses on people.
- The manager relies on control; the leader inspires trust.
- The manager has a short-range view; the leader asks what and why.
- The manager has his/her eye on the bottom line; the leader has his/her eye on the horizon.
- The manager initiates; the leader originates.
- The manager accepts the status quo; the leader challenges it.
- The manager is the classic good soldier; the leader is his/her own person.

As I stated earlier, leadership and management are two notions that are often used interchangeably. However, these words actually describe two different concepts.

Leadership is a facet of management. Leadership is just one of the many assets a successful manager must possess. The main aim of a manager is to maximize the output of the school through administrative implementation. To achieve this managers must undertake the following functions: organization, planning, staffing, directing and controlling. Leadership is just one important component of the directing function. A manager cannot just be a leader, he or she also needs formal authority to be effective (Predpall 1994).

A manager needs a leadership style that acknowledges people as individuals. They need to coach others to peak performance by using empowerment and coaching relationships. This means empowering and motivating teachers and staff to peak performance by responding to employees' human needs with sensitivity and flexibility.

Being able to mold a diverse teaching staff into a cohesive, productive team in today's dynamic schools demands a new type of leadership. The new leader/manager must be visionary change agents, coaches, and empowerers. They must manage change in a positive, proactive way by responding and clearly communicating their expectations, objectives, and goals for the school and its staff. We must learn to manage change and diversity with a leadership style that works to create a productive staff for the school.

Management knows how it works. A manager knows how each layer of the system works and may also possess a good technical knowledge. A leader is often a new arrival to a school who has bold, fresh, and new ideas, but may lack experience and wisdom.

Managers think incrementally, while leaders think radically. Managers do things right while leaders do the right things. This means that managers do things by the book and follow district policies, while leaders follow their own intuition, which may be of more benefit to the school.

Leaders stand out by being different. They question assumption and are suspicious of tradition. They seek out the truth and make the decisions based on fact, not prejudice. Leaders have a preference for innovation (Fenton 1990).

Teaching staff may be more loyal to a leader than a manager. This loyalty is created by the leader taking responsibility in such areas as taking the blame when things go wrong, celebrating group achievements, and giving credit where credit is due. Leaders are observant, sensitive people. They know their team and develop mutual confidence within.

I'm sure that you have heard the comment, "The leader is followed. The manager rules." A leader is someone who the staff will follow through their own choice, whereas a manager must be obeyed. A manager often obtains his or her position of authority through time and loyalty given to the school, not as a result of his or her leadership qualities. A leader may have no organizational skills, but his or her vision unites people behind him or her.

Both leaders and managers must be creative and help unleash the creativity of the staff. What is creativity? A creative thing must be new, unique, or novel. But the solution also has to work. In other words, creativity is novelty that is useful.

There is nothing mysterious about creativity. It is a natural process like breathing or your heartbeat. Nature operates under two basic principles, divergence and convergence. When nature diverges, it generates thousands of unique combinations of plant and animal life. Then through the process of naturalization it converges and chooses for survival the most adaptable species.

To be more creative managers/leaders we can take a lesson from nature. When working to solve a problem or capitalize on an opportunity, first diverge. Stretch your thinking and generate many options. Only after that should you converge and select the best of these options to refine and put into action.

To change our thinking and then to change our behavior requires that we take an honest look at ourselves. When I force myself to honestly look in the mirror, I find things that I really don't want to see. I see that I have been wrong. I see that I've made mistakes. I see that I've hurt people who were important to me. Admitting these mistakes makes me vulnerable and very uncomfortable, yet it is critical to do this if I want to move ahead and succeed in areas where I've failed before.

Take a walk with me for a moment, down the corridor of a major metropolitan art gallery. Look around. We pass paintings by Cézanne, Renoir, Gauguin, and Van Gogh. There is no doubt that our society recognizes these artists as creative. As we look at these paintings most of us don't believe that we could create something so treasured. Most of us don't think of ourselves as creative. Most of us believe that only artists, composers, and inventors are creative. Not true. We are all creative and we all express our creativity in different and valuable ways.

Abraham Maslow, the eminent psychologist, stressed that a first-rate soup is better than a fourth-rate painting (Maslow 1959). In other words, the medium in which you choose to create doesn't matter. The important thing is that you express your creativity in some way that is rewarding to you, and it is hoped, to others.

Most leaders don't work with oil paint, clay, or watercolors. They create with the most complex medium of all—people. My artist friends may take exception to my next comment, but artists have it easy. Paint and clay do not go on strike. Paint and clay do not stomp away in anger. Paint and clay can be "told" what to do and always respond without complaining. Paint and clay never need benefit plans, drug abuse counseling, or days off. People are so much more complicated than inanimate media. It takes tremendous effort and dedication to create with people. However, the dividends can be phenomenal.

Changing things is central to leadership and changing them before anyone else is creativeness.

There are times to be creative and times to follow the routine. If it ain't broke, don't fix it! If you have procedures that are working leave them alone. If I am on an airplane and the pilot is coming in for a routine landing I don't want him and the copilot to brainstorm ways to land the plane. I never want to hear, "Let's see, we could buzz the control tower or we could see how close we could get to those other nice jets." But if a problem came up I would want them to come up with some new solutions. My survival would depend on the pilot's creativity.

How do we begin? How do you, with all your vast and valuable knowledge, invoke the child within you to see the world with a fresh pair of eyes?

Roger Firestien (2001) explores twelve ways to evoke your creativity so you can nurture it in the teachers and the staff who work with you.

1. Develop creativity habits. Clasp your hands in front of you. Which thumb is up, your right or your left? Unclasp your hands and reclasp them, but this time put your opposite thumb on top. How does it feel? What you have just experienced is what a physical habit feels like.

   Are habits bad? Absolutely not! I have a habit of driving on the right side of the road and stopping at red lights. These are good habits. I get pretty upset when someone gets "creative" with me on them.

   Still leaders say our habitual thinking tends to get in the way when we want to create new ideas. Most of us tend to run with the first idea we come up with, even if it causes us to run off the edge of a cliff.

   Managers say that the next time you have a tough problem to solve, ask yourself, "How else can I do this? What if . . . ?"

   The philosopher Socrates has often been paraphrased, "When you always do what you've always done, you always get what you've always got." If you like what you are getting, terrific. If you want changes you need new creative habits. By the way, if the

Socrates phrase doesn't work for you, try this one: "Insanity is do-ing the same thing over and over while expecting different results."

2. Ask questions. Voltaire once said, "Judge a person by his questions rather than his answers." Make sure the questions you ask are open, then be ready to receive an answer. Part of asking questions is not being afraid to appear stupid. Voltaire said of a know-it-all of his generation, "He must be very ignorant, for he answers every ques-tion he asks."

3. Use passive ways to generate ideas. Don't neglect the passive ways to get new ideas that come to you while driving a car, taking a bath or shower, or as you fall asleep at night. The key is to catch these ideas when they appear.

4. Vary your routine. It's no surprise that many of us get great ideas for work-related problems when we are on vacation. We vary our routine. We are not keeping regular hours and are not in a familiar environment. We can adapt the vacation approach by treating our committee time as a scenic vacation. Meet in a different room. Sit in a different chair.

5. Read and listen to a variety of material. "Slugs" read almost noth-ing. "Productive" people read almost exclusively in their field, while "innovative" people read in a variety of fields.

6. Network. Interact with people from varying backgrounds who have a variety of interests.

7. Develop personal support systems. It is critical to have in place the personal and professional relationships that can provide you with a support system when the going gets tough.

8. Stop the action. The peace of solitude is difficult to attain in our culture. We are constantly bombarded with things to do, to buy, and to change. Take time out to meditate, rest, and reflect. It is said that Gandhi spent from midnight on Sunday night to midnight Monday night in solitude, fasting, prayer, and meditation.

9. Create an environment that encourages creativity. Artists and mu-sicians have studios, craftsmen have workshops, professors have offices, and scientists have laboratories. Where is your creative space? Where do you do your best work? My friend Kal, a profes-sional artist, describes her studio as her safe place. When she is in her studio, she is able to create, try out new concepts, and leave her work in progress. It is a place where no one disturbs her. It is her

retreat from the hectic, outside world, a place where she can im-
merse herself in a private world of concepts and colors. My office,
filled with student works of art, is my sanctuary.

10. Create a healthy lifestyle. Exercise causes a person to think more
clearly and to become motivated.

11. Reawaken your sense of humor. Develop a comic vision, model a
sense of humor, and be true to yourself.

12. Be passionate about your positive, compelling, future vision. Work
with teachers to translate that vision into objectives that create specific and measurable results. Managers deal with problems. Managers phrase problems in a way they can be solved. "A problem
properly stated is half solved," says John Dewey.

Albert Einstein was once asked, "If some eminent disaster threatened
the world and you had one hour in which you knew you could save it, how
would you spend your time?" Einstein replied, "I would spend the first
fifty-five minutes identifying the problem and the last five minutes solving it." Einstein was right. If you want your school to succeed, it is crucial to view problems and talk about them in a way they can be solved.
Challenge the problem and don't solve the wrong problem.

Using phrases like, "How might we . . . ?" "How to . . . ?" or "In what
ways might we . . . ?" eases your mind that the problem just might be
solvable.

Defer judgment and generate many ideas. "The best way to have a good
idea is to have lots of ideas," says Linus Pauling, the Nobel Prize winner
for chemistry and peace.

Alex Osborn, founder of the Creative Education Foundation and author
of *Applied Imagination* (1953), developed the following guidelines for
generating ideas:

- Defer judgment. Take time to analyze.
- Strive for equality. The greater the number of ideas, the greater the
likelihood of solving the issue.
- Welcome "free-wheeling." The wilder the idea the better. It is easier
to tame down than to think up.
- Seek combination and improvement. How can the ideas of others be
turned into better ideas? How can two or more ideas be fused into still
another idea?

As a manager I would suggest that we praise and recognize ideas. No stimulus to creative effort is as effective as a good pat on the back. Creativity flourishes in an environment where praise is abundant. Genuine praise has power. It has the muscle to give hope to the discouraged, energy to the feeble, and life to the masses.

We must also learn from mistakes. Living is a risky business. If we spend half as much time learning how to take risks as we spend avoiding them, we wouldn't have so much to fear.

Failure, mistake, fiasco, bomb, dead, flop, turkey, garbage, junk, reject, scrap, setback, breakdown, screw-up, blunder, blooper, foul-up, bungle, faux pas. These are just a few of the words that most of us use when things don't turn out the way we had planned or hoped or imagined. Look closely at those words. They are all value judgments. They describe an outcome of an action in a decidedly negative way.

Whenever you do anything, you create a result. A failure is simply a result that you hadn't anticipated. The expression "trial and error" focuses on unanticipated results that failed. Managers look at failures as learning experiences. They can help us become more successful. Let's change the phrase "trial and error" to "tried and learn."

Thomas Edison experimented with about six thousand ways to invent the light bulb until he finally came up with the filament material that worked for him. Was each one of those initial combinations a failure? No, they just didn't produce the results Edison wanted. Edison was a master at using his mistakes as stepping-stones to discovery. He lived out the maxim proclaimed by Albert Szent-Gyorgyt: "Discovery consists of looking at the same thing as everyone else and thinking something different." Never forget that mistakes can be stepping-stones to success. Encourage your staff to take risks. Reward for effort, don't punish for failure.

FOUR ELEMENTS OF SUCCESSFUL MANAGEMENT

You are busy. You are stressed. One teacher is hammering you with curriculum questions, another is spinning his wheels on a discipline issue, someone else is nagging to change benefits.

Stop, take a breath, and let's get back to business. Fighting fires and struggling to maintain control is not what management is all about. Effective people management boils down to just four fundamental skills: selecting, directing, evaluating, and rewarding. These skills interlock like links in a chain. Get them right and you are guaranteed success. Foul up a single area and your effectiveness will be compromised.

Select

Rather than trying to force fit a good candidate into a vague job slot, define the position and then seek the right person to fill it. Outline the position and responsibilities, conduct ongoing job audits, write job descriptions that set goals and objectives in measurable terms, and then conduct the interviews.

Direct

Nothing works better at moving your teachers and your school toward educational goals than strategic plan-based direction involving parents, teachers, students, and the community. Clear direction benefits your school in the following ways:

- Helps orient new teachers by letting them know what is required
- Creates a can-do attitude
- Creates an exciting culture in which results are measured, milestones are celebrated, and growth is promoted
- Makes it easier to evaluate performance
- Facilitates teamwork
- Reduces difficulties involving personality differences or teacher diversity
- Builds loyalty
- Builds to frequent, visible accomplishments or "little victories" that motivate teachers.

Evaluate

When you've assigned specific tasks, responsibilities, and objectives with deadlines, then evaluation is simply a matter of determining if the teacher has met those goals. Create your own customized evaluation formats, collect meaningful data, and use evaluation to determine a teacher's future role. Evaluation can be intimidating but when selection and direction are done properly, evaluation becomes a logical, easy-to-implement process. The goal of the evaluation process is to make sure that the talents of the teachers are utilized in a way that benefits the school and the teacher.

Reward

Sustaining high levels of performance is not just a matter of proper selection, direction, and evaluation. It also requires appropriate rewards for accomplishments. Pick a reward system that will attract the people you want and get the results you expect. A reward is whatever someone has coming as a result of his or her performance.

Someone once wrote, "To some people life is a dance, to others it is a wrestling match, to the rest it is a jail term." People who feel life is a jail term also never become managers. Their basically negative attitude on almost everything prevents them from being promoted to or striving for a management position. Other people are born wrestlers, but the average person has to be trained in basic wrestling skills. The same is true for managers. It is important that they identify and develop the skills they need. Sometimes managers recognize these skills early on and, other times, a moment of enlightenment suddenly illuminates the fundamentals and they become second nature.

Education is incremental. Enlightenment is not. If you nurture the incremental process of learning, you are depending on enlightenment. You are hoping that you or someone else will eventually find the way. That's not likely to happen and it's not good management.

The purpose of management is to accomplish objectives as quickly as possible at the lowest costs. But because goals and objectives constantly shift and exact cost accounting is impossible or impractical, achieving goals is not easy. To make matters worse, people tend to make things more complicated than they really are by paying too much attention to details. It's better to identify the framework or skeleton that supports a body of work.

In management, as in any endeavor, basic skills must be developed before exceptional performance can be achieved. The wrestler works at developing and maintaining basic holds and moves because, when perfected, they provide the means to deal with the majority of the challenges to be faced. Not doing this will place any wrestler at a real disadvantage against competitors who have mastered the basic elements. Likewise, the managers who develop and polish the four basic elements of effective management (select, direct, evaluate, and reward) will be prepared to match wits and staff against any contender.

What knowledge and skills should principals and school directors put into use in their day-to-day jobs? The Interstate School Leaders Licensure Consortium (ISLLC), a consortium organized by the Council of Chief State School Officers, developed standards to connect the principals' and directors' leadership/management role to student achievement. According to the ISLLC, these research-based standards provide common ground for schools to hire and assess school leaders. In summary form the ISLLC standards call for school administrators to promote the success for all students by:

- Facilitating the development, articulation, implementation, and vision that is shared and supported by the school community
- Advocating, nurturing, and sustaining a school culture and instructional program conductive to student learning and staff professional growth
- Ensuring management of the school's operations and resources for a safe, effective, and efficient learning environment
- Celebrating with families and community members responding to diverse community interests and needs and mobilizing community resources.
- Acting with integrity, fairness, and an ethical manner
- Understanding, responding to, and influencing the larger political, social, economic, legal, and cultural context

School leaders should be very knowledgeable about child and adult development. They should also hold and communicate positions on issues such as testing and grouping students. School leaders also need to be able to handle the requisite give-and-take that occurs among teachers, students, parents, and others during the process of shaping a school to become a true community of learners.

Leaders and managers also need to mold the values, beliefs, and attitudes that are embedded in the school's culture and climate. Principals who scorn parents, treat teachers in a subservient and hostile manner, and break promises are bound to see these types of behaviors and worse creep into the school. Principals who respect others, ask questions, and take advice as well as doing their daily work with honesty and integrity are likely to see similar behaviors reflected throughout the school.

The stories successful leaders and managers tell about their school careers contribute to our knowledge and understanding of leadership, management, and school improvement. The school leaders I interviewed identified key leadership ingredients that fit into five categories:

1. Partnership and voice: cultivating everyone's help and giving everyone an opportunity to participate in genuine change.
2. Vision and values: adopting key beliefs and attitudes that are shared throughout the school community, and for leaders and managers, being what they call "keepers of the dream."
3. Knowledge and daring: including risk taking, pushing boundaries, and increasing the capacity for all staff to make good decisions.
4. Savvy and persistence: knowing how the system works, being able to "take a lot of flak," and maintaining a network of support.
5. Personal qualities: including dedication and passion, empathy, patience, wisdom, common sense, reliability, and humor (a trait leaders and managers consider priceless).

But if these school leaders and managers take a wide view of leadership, one that encompasses the entire community, and stretches broadly and deeply into every aspect of their school, they also take time to look inward. They need to assess their own leadership and managerial skills. This requires introspection in the form of reflective journals, meetings with mentors who serve as "critical friends," and a review of data collected from surveys and performance rubrics. Strong leaders need to know when to attach the close-up lens and scrutinize their personal leadership/managerial style and achievements.

Things may be going well, but will it last? Managers fail when they succumb to certain temptations. The following are temptations you should try to resist:

- Status: Some managers make decisions they think will protect their own status, forgetting how they came to be in the position they are.

How to resist: Make results your top priority. Better results help your school.

- Popularity: When managers do not hold their staff accountable for results, they often do so to gain popular support.
  How to resist: Manage for respect, not affection.
- Perfection: Many managers are driven by a need to be correct.
  How to resist: Recognize that part of your job is to take risks. Trust your intuition to support the data you have. When mistakes happen, because they will, discuss them.
- Harmony: Managers may be uncomfortable with debate, so they avoid and discourage it.
  How to resist: Tolerate discord and realize that differences contribute to better decisions.
- Playing it safe: Insecure managers can't tolerate appearing weak. So they avoid controversy. Refusing to take a stand on an issue tells staff you may not stand up for them.
  How to resist: Gain your staff's trust by clearly explaining your actions so they will understand your decisions, whether or not they agree. They're more likely to respect your judgment when they know the reasoning behind it.

Employees fail when they aren't sure what the job is, they don't know how to do the job, or if a person or situation interferes with the employee's ability to do the job. Leaders and managers need to help, coach, and encourage. Try to follow these lessons learned from successful managers:

- Clearly state the goal for the team.
- Approach each individual differently.
- Use mistakes constructively.
- Prepare your team.
- Prepare yourself.
- Have the courage of your convictions.
- Inject humor and excitement into the life of the school.
- Instill loyalty. Be loyal.
- If you do something you love with your life, you will make an impact.

TYPES OF LEADERSHIP

What kind of leader are you? There are three broad leadership strategies that have been researched: hierarchical, transformational, and facilitative. School administrators can mix and match these models according to the needs and circumstances of their schools.

Instructional leadership, a concept that emerged in the 1980s, calls for leaders to set clear expectations, maintain firm discipline, and implement high standards. Instructional leaders today, as then, are judged by the students' academic achievements. This becomes a hierarchical model in which leaders rule their schools with authority and demand that teachers follow their orders for curriculum and instruction. Principals who follow this style tend to spend considerable time supervising and running their buildings in a "top-down" approach.

The advantage of hierarchical leadership is that it is straightforward and predictable, and the results can be efficient and cost-effective. But there is a downside: Leaders who follow this style tend to squelch creativity and turn their relationship with teachers and others into one that has more to do with efficiency than with education.

Transformational strategies, on the other hand, allow leaders to motivate, inspire, and unite teachers and others on common goals. Transformational leaders tend to rely on persuasion, idealism, and intellectual excitement to capture and persuade others to join their vision and share their dreams. Principals and others who attempt to lead by using transformational strategies need a high level of energy and a huge reservoir of knowledge and skills about teaching and learning. However, a school run by an emotional and excited leader doesn't always achieve its goals.

Facilitative leadership puts school leaders at the center of school management, particularly when it comes to adapting to new situations, solving problems, and improving school performance. School leaders who facilitate change involve others, including teachers, support staff, students, and parents, to help make decisions and solve problems. To accomplish goals, facilitative leaders devote time and energy into building teams, creating communication networks, and modeling the school's ideals and vision.

Which kind of leadership works best? Keep the following guidelines in mind as you make "strategic choices" about which leadership strategies best fit your personal style and the needs of your school:

- Use leadership strategies flexibly. Before leaping into a full-blown facilitative style, be sure your school is ready to accept the roles and responsibilities required of administration and teachers.
- Choose leadership strategies according to short-term and long-term needs. For some school functions, such as preparing a budget on time, you might need to use a more hierarchical style, for planning curriculum programs, such as changing a reading or math program, you might be able to use a facilitative approach.
- Select leadership strategies that best serve your school's students. You might need to nip a problem, such as intervening with a teacher who is using inappropriate discipline, with a quick fix that requires decisive action. You might be able to spend more time working collaboratively with community groups to develop intramural sports programs.
- Think of leadership strategies for every action. Consider what type of leadership you will use with lunchroom workers, bus drivers, parents, special education teachers, and so forth. Think of every action as an opportunity to help students, to assess the school's climate, and to reinforce the school's key values.

In sum, managing and leading are two different ways of organizing people. The manager uses a formal, rational method, while the leader uses passion and stirs emotions. William Wallace (1272–1305) is one example of a brilliant leader, but one who could never be thought of as the manager of the Scots. Wallace was a brilliant military strategist who defended Scotland against King Edward I of England during the war of 1297. He used passion for his beloved Scotland and stirred the emotions of the men who followed him to feel the same passion. This is a trait of leadership. He did not use a formal, rational method of fighting as did the English, which is a trait of managers.

ARE MANAGERS LEADERS?

Some think of leadership as being associated with the role of a manager, and use the terms synonymously. However, a manager may not necessarily be a leader and vice versa.

First, let's look at the definition of a leader. Raven and Rubin (1976, 37) define a leader as "[s]omeone who occupies a position in a group, influences others in accordance with the role expectation of the position and coordinates and directs the group in maintaining itself and reaching its goal." Therefore, the term "leadership" would be an expansion of this definition, being the "process of influence between a leader and his followers to attain group organizational and societal goals" (Avery and Baker 1990, 453).

Some forms of leadership exist in all groups, with the central attribute being social influence. The leader is the person who has the most impact on a group's behavior and beliefs. "He or she is the one who initiates action, gives orders, makes decisions, settles disputes between group members, offers encouragement, serves as a model, and is in the fore-front of group activity" (Sears 1988, 400).

Leadership functions are many and varied depending upon the basic issues a school must deal with. The leadership/managerial style is dependent on the basis of power. Power in the case of leadership is divided into five categories, each linked with another as they are interrelated. *Informational power* is concerned with skills, knowledge, and information, of which the holders of such abilities are able to utilize in influencing others. *Reward and coercive power* involve the ability to either reward or punish persons being influenced, in order to gain compliance. *Legitimate power* is power that has been confirmed by the very role structure of the school itself and is accepted by all as correct and without dispute, such as in the case of armed forces or the police force. *Referent power* involves those being influenced identifying with the leader—that is, rock or film personalities using their image to enter the political arena (Marshall 1999).

Most leaders and managers make use of a combination of these five types of power depending on the leadership style used. Authoritarian leaders, for example, use a mixture of legitimate, coercive, and reward powers to dictate the policies, plans, and activities of a school. In comparison, a democratic or participative leader would use mainly referent power, involving all members of the school in the decision-making process.

LEADERS VERSUS MANAGERS

Most people view leadership as being associated with the role of a manager. However, there are some who suggest that leaders and managers are not equal positions. As previously mentioned, leading and managing involve separate and distinct behaviors and activities. Leaders and managers, these sources continue, vary in their orientation toward goals, conceptions about teaching, interpersonal style, and self-perceptions.

> Leaders . . . are often dramatic and unpredictable in style. They tend to create an atmosphere of change, even chaos. They are often obsessed by their ideas, which appear as visionary and consequently excite, stimulate and drive others to work hard to create reality out of fantasy. . . . [M]anagers are typically hardworking, analytical, tolerant, and fair-minded. They have a strong sense of belonging to the organization, and take great pride in perpetuating and improving the status quo. (French 1987, 475)

It must be pointed out that a manager may not necessarily be a team leader. While a manager of a team performs activities of a planning, organizing, and controlling nature, the real leader may be one of his or her subordinates.

In contrast, an opposing view states that leadership is just one aspect of what a manager does. Vecchio, Hearn, and Southey assert that managers fulfill four functions: planning, organizing, controlling, and leading. This leading aspect of management involves influencing subordinates toward the achievement of the school's goals.

> Leadership thus implies something more than a mere supervisory responsibility or formal authority. It consists of influence that accompanies legitimacy as a supervisor. Therefore, it can be said that leadership is the incremental influence that a person has beyond his/her formal authority. Incremental influences can exist to varying degrees in every member of the team. As a result, it is not uncommon to find situations in which a subordinate who lacks formal authority, actually possesses substantial incremental influence. We would call such an individual an informal leader. (Vecchio, Hearn, and Southey 1988, 334)

These informal leaders often possess abilities the appointed manager may lack, such as technical expertise or articulate communication skills. Thus leadership can exist on a formal or informal basis, an additional distinction from management.

Leadership clearly entails more than wielding power and exercising authority. However, it is difficult to ascertain whether managers are leaders or not.

Table 2.1.   Traits of Managers and Leaders

Manager Traits	Leader Traits
Doesn't ensure imagination, creativity, or ethical behavior.	Uses personal power to influence the thoughts and actions of others.
Rationally analyzes a situation, developing systematic selection of goals and purposes (what is to be done).	Intuitive, mystical understanding of what needs to be done.
Directs energy toward: goals, resources, organization structure, determining the problems to be solved.	Directs energy in guiding people toward practical solutions.
Perpetuates group conflicts.	Works to develop harmonious interpersonal relationships.
Becomes anxious when there is relative disorder.	Works best when things are somewhat disorderly or chaotic.
Uses her accumulation of collective experience to get where she is going.	Often jumps to conclusions, without a logical progression of thoughts or facts.
Innovates by "tinkering" with existing processes.	Innovates through flashes of insight or intuition.
Sees the world as relatively impersonal and static (black and white).	Sees the world as full of color, and constantly blending into new colors and shapes.
Influences people through the use of logic, fact, and reason.	Influences people through altering moods, evoking images, and expectation.
Views work as an enabling process, involving a combination of ideas, skills, timing, and people.	Views work as developing fresh approaches to old problems, or finding new options for old issues.
Views work as something that must be done or tolerated.	Views work as something challenging and exciting.
Has an instinct for survival; seeks to minimize risks and tolerate the mundane.	Sometimes reacts to the mundane and routine as an affliction.
Has a low level of emotional involvement in her work.	Takes in emotional signals from others, making them mean something in the relationship with an individual; often passionate about her work.
Relates to people by the role she plays in a sequence or in a decision-making process.	Relates to people in intuitive and empathetic ways.
Focuses on how things need to be done.	Focuses on what needs to be done, leaving decisions to people involved.
Focuses attention on procedure.	Focuses on decisions to be made.
Communicates with subordinates indirectly, using "signals."	Communicates through "messages," heightening the emotional response.
Once-born; her life has been most straightforward and predictable; takes things for granted.	Twice-born; her life has not always been easy, often marked by some struggle to attain a sense of order; does not take things for granted.

(continued)

Table 2.1. Traits of Managers and Leaders (*continued*)

Manager Traits	Leader Traits
Sees herself as a conservator and regulator of an existing order of affairs; belongs to the organization; believes in duty and responsibility to her organization.	Sees herself as separate from her environment; may work in organizations but never belongs to them; searches for opportunities for change.
Sees herself as an integral part of their social structure and social standard.	Sees herself as a constantly evolving human being, focusing more inwardly than outwardly.
Develops herself through socialization, seeking to maintain the balance of social relations.	Develops herself through personal mastery, struggling for psychological and social change.
Finds harmony in living up to society's, the company's, and her family's expectations.	Finds self-esteem through self-reliance and personal expression.
Forms moderate and widely distributed personal attachments with others.	Forms intensive one-on-one relationships that may be of short duration; often has mentors.

SKILLS MANAGERS REQUIRE

We have talked about managers needing management and leadership skills to manage a school successfully. These two broad categories encompass many detailed skills.

Skill development is a process of academic learning, coaching, mentoring, hands-on training, and the opportunity to try to learn from different job experiences over time. Each school experiences different problems at different times in its development. The need for experience over time is invaluable in the development of a manager.

Technical skills refer to the ability to understand and use knowledge, techniques, and tools that are used in the performance of specific tasks.

Leadership skills are people skills. Grace Hooper, American Admiral, once said, "You don't manage people, you manage things. You lead people." The manager's ability to work effectively with and through people is critical to the management process. Staff will follow a leader when the leader excites them with a purpose, an attainable goal. The manager must respect the staff's talents and involve them in planning and the operational process. Remember, no one knows more about the job than the person doing it. These interpersonal skills take time to develop and come from creating an atmosphere of mutual respect between management and staff.

The staff must understand the communication of the manager and not misunderstand intentions. Good communication requires a sender and a receiver who are on the same wavelength. Communication is verbal and nonverbal. The nonverbal sends a more powerful message.

Management is a stepping-stone process in which you solve problems when your school experiences them. All managers need to have five basic skills—leadership skills, communication skills, technical skills, human relations skills, and conceptual skills—in varying degrees. Management requires that you conceptualize the problem-solving process and the interrelationship of its individual parts.

Management skill development is a twofold, life-long learning experience. Increase your personal skills and continue your academic education. Train yourself through dedication and hard work.

Let's now compare the changing styles of managers and leaders as we move into the new millennium.

CHANGING STYLES FOR THE NEW MILLENNIUM

Changing styles for leaders and managers for the new millennium include several qualities that are important for a person who will be both a manager and a leader. These qualities include empowerment, restructure, teaching, role modeling, openness, and the ability to acknowledge questions and answers. The following table reflects these changing styles. Both leading and managing are desired aspects in directing a school. Both need to be present in order for the school to become an efficient and effective organization. Individual styles are necessary for success in the awesome school.

Before we conclude this chapter let us take a brief look at Peter Drucker, the guru of management, and see how he relates to education today. In his book *Management Challenges for the Twenty-first Century*, Drucker discusses the new paradigms of management and how they have changed and will continue to change our basic assumptions about the practices and principles of management. Drucker analyzes the new realities of strategy, shows how to be a leader in periods of change, and explains the "New Information Revolution," discussing the information a manager needs and the information a manager owes.

Table 2.2. **Changing Styles for the New Millennium**

Moving from Management	*Moving toward Leadership*
Quality: Empowerment	
Punishment	Reward
Demands "respect"	Invites speaking out
Drill sergeant	Motivator
Limits and defines	Empowers
Imposes discipline	Values creativity
"Here's what we are going to do!"	"How can I serve you?"
Bottom line	Vision
Quality: Restructure	
Control	Change
Rank	Connection
Hierarchy	Network
Rigid	Flexible
Automatic annual raises	Pay for performance
Performance review	Mutual contract for results
Mechanistic	Holistic
Compartmental	Systemic
Quality: Teaching	
Order-giving	Facilitating
Military archetype	Teaching archetype
Quality: Role Model	
Issues orders	Acts as a role model
Demands unquestioning obedience	Coaches and mentors others
Quality: Openness	
Keeping people on their toes	Nourishing environment for growth
Reach up/down	Reach out
Information control	Information availability
Quality: Questions and Answers	
Knows all the answers	Asks the right questions
Not interested in new answers	Seeks to learn and draw out new ideas

Drucker has related his management strategies to enhance management in schools. The ideas that follow are directly related to Drucker's management philosophy.

The school must be transparent. Teachers have to know and understand the school structure they are supposed to work in. Someone in the school must have the authority to make the final decision. And someone must clearly be in command in a crisis.

One does not "manage" people. The task is to lead people. The goal is to make productive the specific strengths and knowledge of each individual.

Management exists for the sake of the school's results. It has to start with the intended results and has to organize the resources of the school to attain these results. The goal is to make the school capable of producing results outside of itself.

Strategy allows a school to be purposefully opportunistic, allowing for creativity and change.

Japan is one among very few countries that understands that the crucial element in a country's ability to perform is the education of the small child, and that the elementary schoolteacher is the most important part of the educational establishment and needs to be respected as such. School leaders and managers in the United States would do well to respect and value their teachers and realize they are also responsible for results.

One cannot manage change, one can only be ahead of it. In times of change, it is the *learners* who inherit the future. The *learned* usually find themselves equipped to live in a world that no longer exists.

Starve problems and feed opportunities. Don't confuse novelty with innovation. The test of an innovation is that it creates value. A novelty only creates amusement.

Drucker finds that difficulty arises in defining what the task is and what it should be. A good example of this is the American school. Public schools in the American inner city have become disaster areas. But next to them, in the same location and serving the same kind of children, are private (mostly Christian) schools in which the kids behave well and learn well. There is endless speculation to explain these enormous quality differences. But a major reason surely is that the two kinds of schools define their tasks differently. The typical public school defines its task as "helping the underprivileged." The typical Christian schools (and especially the parochial schools of the Catholic Church) define their task as "enabling those who want to learn, to learn." One is governed by its scholastic failures, the other by its scholastic successes.

The very great achievers—Napoleon, da Vinci, Mozart—have always managed themselves. But they were the rarest of exceptions. And they were unique, both in their talents and in their achievements, and considered to be outside the boundaries of normal human existence. Now even people of modest endowments—that is, average mediocrity—will have to learn to manage themselves in order to achieve success.

As we face new demands we ask: What are my strengths?

Most people think that they know what they are good at. They are usually wrong. People know what they are *not* good at. And yet, one can only perform with one's strengths. One cannot build performance on weakness, let alone on something one cannot do at all. Following are some questions to ask yourself as you analyze your strengths and weaknesses.

How do I perform? Amazingly few people know how they get things done. The teacher who ran a classroom of forty youngsters simply did not have the time to find out how each of the students performed. The teacher had to insist that all do the same work, the same way, at the same time. And so historically everyone grew up with one way of doing the work. Currently, new technology has enabled teachers to find out how a student learns and then encourages the student to do the work the way that fits the individuals learning style.

How do I learn? Schools everywhere are organized on the assumption that there is one right way to learn, and that is the same way for everybody. Many first-class writers—Winston Churchill is but one example—do poorly in school, and they tend to remember their school as pure torture. Their classmates may not have enjoyed the school experience either, but the worst they suffered was boredom. The explanation is that first-rate writers do not, as a rule, learn by listening and reading. They learn by writing. Since this is not the way the school allows them to learn, they get poor grades. To be forced to learn the way the school teaches is sheer hell for them. Do not try to change yourself, but work hard to improve the way you perform.

What are my values? To be effective in a school as a leader or manager, one's own values must be compatible with the school's values. They do not need to be the same, but close enough to coexist.

Where do I belong? In other words, who am I?

What is my contribution? To ask this means moving from knowledge to action.

What is my relationship responsibility? Most people work with other people and are effective through other people. When we tap into people's basic moral and ethical beliefs, we accomplish much more than when we facilitate some carefully crafted, well-timed, and professionally correct encounter.

Success comes far more readily (and far more frequently) when you think, evaluate, and plan before you act.

Successful managers encourage observations as well as the use of strategies. Consider the following:

- Innovative solutions result from thinking "outside the box."
- Knowledge and information are power.
- Make decisions on how things actually are, rather than how you hope they will be, or how others are presenting them to you.
- To help teachers achieve optimal performance, be flexible and tolerant in nurturing their skills. Some simple attention to the needs of staff and a willingness to treat them like the valuable assets they are can go a long way toward solving and preventing a variety of problems.
- To be successful, give your school a clear future.
- Take control of circumstances or they will take control of you.
- Effective leaders adapt their management approach to best suit their particular situation.
- Proactivity, flexibility, and innovation are three of the best tools that any manager can wield.

Has your school survived a major initiative only to be ambushed by another theory that demands that you rush full speed in the opposite direction? Have you been told that the fate of education depends on the search for excellence, quality, or assessment? Do you dream of the day the consultants will go away and let you get back to work?

The irony is that some of the management ideas and prescriptions really can rescue or renovate your school. The key is to determine which ideas belong in your hot file and which in your circular file. Remember the words of Victor Hugo: "You can resist an invading army. You cannot resist an idea whose time has come."

Close study indicates that management remains an art rather than a science. Consider the following:

- Only the paranoid survive.
- When considering a new idea, ask yourself: Is it intelligible? Does it add more than mere common sense? Is it relevant?
- Thrive on chaos.
- Think up ideas, then sell them.
- Thrive on anxiety.

- Self-discipline only operates when people trust each other.
- Good judgment is the result of experience and experience is the result of bad judgment.
- Have a passion for experimentation and a willingness to fail.

Unleashing this hidden power is not much good unless you know where you wish to go with it. Look to the future.

Many feel that while management and leadership are both important, leadership must come first. You must have a direction before you can intelligently decide which management systems, structures, and controls will best get you there. Leadership defines what the future will look like, aligns people with that vision, and inspires them to make it happen in spite of obstacles.

If I were to put it in a nutshell the major difference between managers and leaders is this: Managers run their schools as though things will always remain the same and leaders run theirs as though everything will change. Leaders move quickly, seize opportunities, take risks, empower others to act, change on a dime, communicate more clearly, and work toward common team goals. Managers are adept at maintaining things, keeping them humming along. Leaders change before they have to, gaining competitive advantage and momentum.

Leadership is developed, not discovered. Managers can upgrade their leadership skills to balance out their management mind-set and thus develop to their fullest potential.

Managers focus on the weaknesses of people and organizations, leaders focus on strengths. This is one of the key differences between how managers and leaders think and act. Managers are forever trying to repair the weaknesses in their people. The problem is that you will rarely turn a weakness into a strength. When you identify strengths you gain momentum, create confidence, and dictate the pace. When you constantly work on weaknesses, you are always playing catch up. Play to your weaknesses and you play to survive. Play to your strengths and you play to win, win often, win big, and win it all.

Managers spend their time charting results; leaders spend their time charting the course. Managers spend too much time and energy looking at and dwelling on the past. Leaders glance at the future. Learn from the past, study it for a moment, and move on.

As you can see, managers and leaders are very different animals. It is important to remember that there are definite strengths and weaknesses in both types of individuals. Managers are very good at maintaining the status quo and adding stability and order to our culture. However, they may not be as good at integrating change and envisioning the future. On the other hand, leaders are very good at steering people's emotions, raising their expectations, and taking them in new directions (both good and bad). However, like artists and other gifted people, leaders often suffer from neuroses and have a tendency toward self-absorption and preoccupation.

Directors and principals in schools must develop management skills whether they come naturally or not. They must also develop leadership qualities. Throughout history, it has been shown again and again that leaders have needed strong one-on-one relationships with teachers whose strengths lie in cultivating talent in order to reach their full potential. I suggest that you find a teacher that you admire, someone who you can connect with and who can help you develop your natural talents and interests. Whether you reach "glory" status or not you will grow in ways you never imagined. Isn't that what life is all about?

Managers, we can surmise, can in certain situations be leaders. However, leadership is only one aspect of their function. Some people have the capacity to become excellent managers, but not strong leaders. Others have great leadership potential, but for a number of reasons, have great difficulty becoming strong managers. Both leading and managing are desired aspects for a principal or director in a school.

A quote from John Kotter (1991, 73) summarizes points already highlighted:

> Leadership is different from management but not for the reason most people think. Leadership is not mystical and mysterious. It has nothing to do with charisma or other exotic personality traits. It is not the providence of a chosen few. Nor is leadership better than management or a replacement for it. Rather, leadership and management are two distinctive and complimentary activities. Both are necessary in an increasingly complex and volatile school environment.

3

The Walk through Your School

In times of change, it is the learners who inherit the future. The learned usually find themselves equipped to live in a world that no longer exists.

—Author Unknown

Educators and teachers are hopeful that despite the pressures that swirl around them they can find strong and loyal friends in their communities. Educators, families, and community members need to reinvigorate the language, social relations, and politics of schooling. It has become a cliché to say that these are precarious times for public schools, but it is also a reality. On the one hand, improving schools is the public's top priority. On the other hand, significant numbers of Americans are giving up on public schools. We must all take a walk through our schools and determine the current status of the educational programs within those schools. To do this we must look at school boards, school report cards, and the conscience and ethics of American youth as we plan for schoolwide reform.

One-size-fits-all school improvement models don't work. Effective reform builds on general school improvement principles and grows out of school leadership and management.

Some general school improvement principles apply to all schools and grade levels. Teacher and administrative quality is by far the most significant factor in school improvement. Research shows that the top one-third of teachers can produce as much as six times the improvement in student achievement as the bottom third (Haycock 1998).

Aligning curriculum to standards and assessment is essential. Educators must also increase students' time on task by using such techniques as providing extra help and mentoring and by insuring that teachers sustain instruction until the end of each class period.

Schools should implement improvement principles that are specific to particular grade spans. In grades K–3 the most powerful improvement principles, especially for minority students, are teaching reading in kindergarten and substantially reducing class size for one year. In grades seven and eight the most powerful improvement principle is helping students understand abstract ideas and symbols and practicing metacognition. In grades 9–12, reducing school size to provide opportunity for more individualized student mentoring is effective.

Schools must also use targeted interventions to meet students' special learning needs. For example, instruction in phonemic awareness does not work for some students because they have trouble accurately hearing sounds.

The biggest impediment to the substantive implementation of these and other improvement principles, however, has been the push for schools to adopt comprehensive schoolwide reform models. Having a vendor take over the curriculum and staff development for a school and provide a one-size-fits-all model is much simpler than struggling to implement these improvement principles. True leadership occurs when a school gets its own act together instead of looking for an outside savior to take control of its basic professional functions and provide a quick fix. A quick fix does not exist.

The best approach is for schools to develop their own internal expertise and leadership for evaluation, curriculum, and instruction, with some outside help on focused, technical, and specialized needs. Education should use a variety of techniques developed from instinct, judgment, and shared experience.

Most important, educators should not implement any improvement principles to the exclusion of individual creativity, initiative, and experimentation. Good teaching is still, at its heart, an artistic endeavor.

Amid the talk of dramatic school reform and restructuring we must remember that the causes of students' poor academic performances are fundamental. We must insure that all students have access to good teachers.

What teachers should know is that educational demographics enter into the picture. Nothing is distributed evenly across the United States—not race, not religion, not age, not fertility, not wealth, and certainly not access to education. Many teachers find they have a classroom of twenty-two in the fall and twenty-two in the following spring, but twenty of those twenty-two are different students. On the average, twenty students have moved away, changed to another school, or even dropped out. Twenty new students from different cultures, demographic areas, and economic backgrounds have replaced the original student make-up of the classroom.

The inner suburban ring (where there is nothing between you and the city limits) will see a major increase in student diversity, more minorities, more immigrants, more students learning English as a second language, and more students from poverty. The second suburban ring (with one suburb between you and the city) will see some decreased diversity in students.

Remember, public schools have mirrored the social transformations of our modern era. If a student is Hispanic or Asian, make sure that you know which country the student's family is from. Mexico, Peru, and Belize are different cultures. Japan, China, and Korea are different cultures. Learn about the cultures. If a student won't look you in the eye, don't make a big issue out of it. Value all students, don't become "color blind." Make all of your goals culturally fair, If you have lots of diversity in your classroom, try to use as many different visual presentations as possible.

Leaders and managers find themselves considering inclusion, multiculturalism, full-day kindergarten, and character education to enhance their programs.

As we walk through our schools we see leadership urging our teachers to "teach our kids to be good." We must do a better job at managing the learning environment. In *Building Character in Schools*, character education experts Kevin Ryan and Karen Bohlen (1999) outline strategies for providing strong moral instruction:

- Let everyone know what you are doing.
- Work toward getting the commitment from everyone. Then seize opportunities to celebrate, model, communicate, and teach virtues and values everywhere, from the lavatories to the playing fields.
- Acknowledge virtuous behavior, but don't always jump in with rewards. Students will learn more from the examples adults set than from posters, slogans, and other gimmicks.

- Allow staff-development time so teachers can learn to bring character education into the curriculum and classroom routines. "Feed the teachers so they won't eat the students."
- Look for moral lessons in every class, but do not reduce any class to the search for a moral lesson. Stories are rich in artistic, literary, and philosophic value.
- Understand the difference between debating moral dilemmas and absorbing moral lessons. Encourage students to be intellectually honest, to gather facts, respect others, and remain humble.

EFFECTIVE AND INEFFECTIVE SCHOOL BOARDS

The current status of schools involves the world of school boards. What an area thriving with leadership and management! We find good boards and bad boards. From clear thinkers to loose cannons, it takes all kinds of people to make a school board. Boards are needed to oversee the accountability and direction a school is moving—the board members and their visions and philosophies will move the school on the path to improvement.

Being a school board member is one of the most difficult jobs in the world. Research concludes that good board members are hard-working members of an educational team who have a deep abiding love for children. Bad board members tend to have personal agendas.

How can you do the good and eschew the bad? Interviews with several school board members resulted in the following ten "good conduct" rules:

1. Effective board members are team players. They work with everyone, supporting the staff and having faith and trust in the leaders they employ. Teachers and administrators need room to experiment, to be innovative. They need to have confidence that their efforts will be respected and encouraged.
2. Effective board members visit the schools. They talk to teachers, students, parents, and administrators.
3. Effective board members, like good teachers and good parents, listen. Many board members hear, but good ones listen. Effective members filter information, separate fact from opinion, and come to strong conclusions. Ineffective board members can't or won't separate issues.

4. Effective board members represent parents and still maintain a professional distance and objectivity. A board must respect the impulse to protect and at the same time listen to staff members and stand behind them and behind school policies.

5. Effective board members are consistent and reliable—they agree with the saying, "have policy, will follow." To be reliable as well as consistent, members must do their homework. Bad members don't. They don't read their reports. They don't pay attention in meetings. They don't talk to staff and they don't make informed decisions.

6. Effective board members are optimists. They believe in what they are doing, and they see light at the end of the tunnel. As one board member said, "I am often depressed about finances, but I am always excited about what we can do."

7. Effective board members support board decisions and still retain their individuality. Effective members can dialogue during the meeting and present a united front at the end. Ineffective board members attack each other rather than the issues.

8. Effective board members communicate honestly, directly, and efficiently with all constituents. A conscientious public servant has to be available to listen to and answer questions for the families, community members, and especially the students.

9. Effective board members have an investment in education. Everyone has an investment in turning out well-educated, employable citizens.

10. Effective board members support students. Outstanding board members create and follow an agenda for children, not an agenda for adults.

That's it! Ten rules that will make your school board more enjoyable and more productive. Board members are taking brave steps to represent their community, allowing everyone to benefit and do their job well.

SCHOOL REPORT CARDS

As managers and leaders walk through a program they are preparing a school report card. The report card helps you tell your own school's story and tell it well.

"We must empower parents with more information and more choices. In too many communities, it's easier to get information on the quality of local restaurants than on the quality of local schools." This comment was made by President Clinton during his 1999 State of the Union address.

Managers stress using school report cards as an opportunity to build public support, a way to increase community confidence that the schools are being held accountable for improving student achievement.

What will you report? Research relates that educators are on a different wavelength from parents and taxpayers.

Instead of hierarchical management, here's what I am going to tell you to do: turn the tables, and start by asking your key stakeholders some simple questions. What counts? What do you need to see to be persuaded that schools are improving? What performance indicators will the public want to know about?

Be prepared to report more than test scores. Statistics on safety and discipline ranked highest, followed by teacher qualifications and test scores. At the same time, do not overload people with too much data. Use the onion peel approach. Provide an easy to read and brief two-page report. But be prepared to offer more information to those who want to peel back the surface layers to get down to the core of the data.

Finally, help people understand how to use the information. You have to know where you are and where you want to go if you are going to improve. You have to be accountable for results.

Educators are asking the question, "Will baby boomers (seventy million of them) maintain their interest in public schools after their kids have left the system? Innovative leadership and management will need creative plans to keep them interested.

Unless public schools become the architects of change, they will become the victims of change. We must attract educators who are competent and responsive to the students' individual needs.

We need public schools that truly belong to the public, and schools that citizens know, understand, and support.

As we walk through schools today we must see the principal who takes the time to pat a teacher on the back, to see a principal pause to dry the eyes of a frightened child. This educator is an example of an effective leader. We must go a step beyond; as with children, positive encouragement is a magic formula for parents and teachers.

SITE-BASED MANAGEMENT

As we walk through many schools we see site-based management. This involves decentralizing decision making and strong leadership by principals and department chairpersons.

Site-based management is often seen as a kind of miracle drug for ailing schools and a tonic for making good schools better.

There is a basic tenet to think about. Those who know best how to educate are the people who know the students best—teachers, principals, parents, and neighbors. Therefore, each campus or school community should have some flexibility to determine the needs of its students and implement staffing patterns, spending plans, and programs and services that fill those needs.

Success depends on making each element of the school community feel as if it has a contribution to make and that it will be listened to.

Not surprisingly, some principals find power sharing too much of a challenge. Some teachers, especially those with hard-earned professional credentials, find the idea of parents in power too foreign a concept. Parents need to learn a lot more about school operation before they can be effective on school site councils and committees.

Look around. Success stories abound in Austin, Texas, Chicago, Illinois, Miami, Florida, Los Angeles, California, and New York City. In these cities, schools see the principal become an advocate and a partner. Parents climb aboard in all areas from maintenance to academics. Teachers become leaders.

Site-based schools often show real gains. Teachers, parents, and leaders have found these schools better able to engage the intellectual and emotional lives of students and to improve academics.

Student learning is not about a single test, on a single day, at one grade level. Students see how their learning in the classroom and in the school community is connected to their lives and is valued by the community around them.

Site-based management takes a new look at contracts between members. There are some established guidelines:

- Write the contract in plain English.
- Spell out details of services to be performed.

- Define your terms.
- Include a complete description of the standards of performance that will be expected and the process you will use to monitor that contract and then evaluate performance.
- Consider using a one- or two-year base contract with additional option years.
- Make sure you have an escape clause.
- Build in flexibility. Things may change.

Let your contracts bridge the gap between management and employees.

As we walk through our schools we need to see administration, leadership, and management supporting and mopping up at the same time. We need to stress the fourth and fifth Rs, respect and responsibility.

Do the students know the meaning of respect? Do our students know the meaning of right and wrong? In addition to the fact that Johnny still can't read, we are now faced with the more serious problem that Johnny can't tell right from wrong.

At one point I asked a student in my class to examine his conscience and relate what he knew about an incident; the student asked, "What is a conscience?"

It is a question a lot of kids in a lot of schools could be asking these days. Children have a hard time telling right from wrong. "What is the difference between cooperative learning and cheating? Between building a lasting relationship and having sex too soon? Between standing up for your rights and punching, or even pulling a gun on someone?" And are any of these things (watch out, here comes a word usually avoided in polite circles) *wrong*?

No one who has picked up a newspaper in this decade doubts the moral crisis in our public schools. Never mind that a similar crisis exists in society at large. School shootings grab headlines, but cheating probably best shows how routine the ethical erosion has become. Seven out of ten high school students admit to cheating according to the "1998 Report Card on the Ethics of American Youth," released in October 1998 by the Josephson Institute of Ethics in Marina del Rey, California.

Sometimes it seems this new generation is bent on self-destruction. Before you dismiss this as the centuries-old complaint of the old against the young, consider the statistics: nationwide, the number of children arrested for murder continues to drop, and the suspects' ages continue to drop. The United States Center for Disease Control and Prevention in Atlanta, Georgia, estimates one million teens become pregnant every year and three million are diagnosed with sexually transmitted diseases. More kids admit to carrying guns, drinking alcohol, smoking marijuana, and using hard drugs than a generation ago.

There is more self-centered behavior on the part of kids. They cheat more, they lie more, they kill one another more. They are more sexually exploited. This self-centeredness has produced little joy. Teen suicides have more than tripled since the 1960s. I think we are going to look back on this period we are going through and think, "What in the world were we doing?" One thing is certain: We, as adults, haven't been doing enough to help kids develop consciences we can live with.

Developmental psychologists say a child's conscience begins forming within the first weeks of life when a baby "attaches" to its caregiver. This is a precursor to developing empathy, the ability to think about other people's feelings.

Adults need to take the lead and encourage kids to think about the consequence of their behavior at a very early age.

Are we preaching? Preaching is a distant second to practicing when it comes to instilling values. Preaching about the effects of school boards, school report cards, the conscience and ethics of American students, site-based management, and the value of parents and community input is a part of life when it comes to making schools better.

4

The Tangled Web: Finances

Any enterprise is built by wise planning, becomes strong through common sense, and profits wonderfully by keeping abreast of the facts.

—Proverbs 24:3–4

Slicing the school finance pie fairly is a lot more complicated than it sounds. Equity in public school funding is like motherhood and apple pie—it's hard to find anyone who is against it. The concept seems simple and unarguable, but in fact, school finance equity is deceivingly complex—a point that is lost in the public policy debates in state legislatures, local cafés, and everywhere in between.

Most people have a narrow view of school finance equity, focusing on getting more money for their own school and giving little or no thought to the resulting effects on other schools or taxpayers. Such a view hinders efforts to increase the equity of school funding at a time when additional financial resources are becoming scarce.

What do we mean by the term equity? Although it is similar in meaning to equality, equity differs in that it does not require strict adherence to the principle of equal treatment for all. Instead equity necessitates fair and just treatment, which, surprising as it may sound, might actually require unequal treatment of some individual or groups. One way of thinking about this issue is to consider three kinds of school finance equity: horizontal equity, vertical equity, and equal opportunity.

The principle of horizontal equity calls for equal spending among students. It assumes that all students have equal educational needs. This becomes an obvious weakness. We know that educational needs vary substantially among students and that there can be considerable cost differences among communities in providing identical educational programs. Thus, horizontal equity is most appropriately applied to subgroups of students where we know that the educational needs and costs are roughly the same.

Given that the needs and costs vary among students and communities, when is unequal funding equitable? Under the principle of vertical equity, disparities in school funding are considered equitable when they are due to factors considered to be legitimately related to educational needs. Such factors may be linked to the characteristics of individual students, districts, or educational programs. Among the student factors considered educationally relevant are learning disabilities, physical and severe mental handicaps, and poor preschool preparation resulting from living in poverty. Some characteristics, however, such as small school enrollment, are not accepted as legitimate vertical equity factors among all policy makers.

Widely applied in evaluating the equity of state school finance plans, the principle of equal opportunity focuses on unjust differences among expenditures. The equal opportunity principle maintains that the distribution of resources should not result in funding disparities that arise from illegitimate factors such as wealth, social class, race, or gender. An aspect of this principle receiving considerable attention is fiscal neutrality, which calls for there to be no relationship between the local wealth of a district and its per pupil expenditures. Fiscal neutrality is rooted in the belief that the quality of education a child receives should be based on the resources of an entire state, rather than solely on those of the community in which the child happens to live.

The biggest hurdle to overcome in all areas of equity is the apathy of many citizens who are happy with the status quo and fail to see any need to change the way schools are funded. School finance equity is a complicated proposition, but understanding it is vital to our efforts to educate all children. We cannot tolerate a system that educates some students very well and others poorly. The interests of all children must be considered when creating school finance systems. The words of Garrison Keillor seem somewhat appropriate for elected officials to consider. "Sometimes you have to set your principles aside and do the right thing."

STRATEGIES

Part of the tangled web relating to finances is making sure leaders and managers plug into energy savings for their schools. Your schools can save money on heating and lighting.

Consider the following scenario:

John quietly enters a classroom where students are working on computers. He flips off the lights and waits to see whether anyone protests. No one moves until five minutes later when he flips the lights back on. Then the students complain, "Leave them off! Leave them off!" The kids could see their computer screens better without the glare, and the expense, of artificial lighting.

Like many of us in the energy conservation movement, John has learned that schools can cut their utility bills without forcing kids to shiver and squint in cold, dark classrooms. Public and private K–12 schools spend more than $6 billion a year on energy cuts, or approximately $110 per student per year. Utility bills are the second largest expense (after personnel costs) and certainly much more than is spent on textbooks. It is the one cost that can be controlled without damaging the quality of the educational program. Schools need to be encouraged to choose more energy-efficient lighting, insulation, windows, and heating and air conditioning systems. But some of the biggest savings come from changing the way people use energy in buildings, which means changing the behavior of the people themselves. We need to encourage energy-wise habits in students, teachers, and everyone in the school.

The following are eight small steps to big energy savings:

1. Turn off the lights. Lighting accounts for over 50 percent of the electric bill in most schools, which means that the oldest and simplest conservation tip is still one of the best. Turn off lights when rooms are empty. Put light switches where people can find them and operate them. Of course schools should not reduce lighting below the standards needed for student learning. Research shows standardized

test scores improve when kids work under natural light. A study of North Carolina elementary school students found that kids who transferred to a new school with daylight outperformed their old classmates by 5 percent on achievement tests after one year and by 14 percent after three years. Students who moved to a school without such daylight did not show similar improvement.

2. Involve the whole school. One person or one class cannot make a noticeable impact on energy use in a school. The savings add up when the entire school joins together in conservation efforts. Schools with effective conservation programs have reported reductions of as much as 25 percent in utility bills. Students can do their own research. One school targeted landscaping as an energy-conservation method. Students researched landscape designs on the Internet, consulted local nurseries to determine appropriate plant species for protecting walls and windows from heat and glare, and involved their local communities in "planting days" aimed at increasing energy efficiency. When staff and students are knowledgeable about energy use and conservation another benefit emerges—they are more likely and willing to spot and report operational problems early on, before costs start to mount. Kids are quick to spot and close outside doors carelessly left open. An underlying goal is to actively involve and empower building users. Students, maintenance staff, teachers, administration, staff, and even interested parents should be part of the team. Once the entire community gets aboard, creative solutions start to flow.

3. Show them the money. Return a portion of the energy savings back to the school as an incentive. Schools can then use a share of the savings to buy supplies, supplementary materials, and books.

4. Don't blow hot and cold. It's expensive to heat and cool buildings, but indoor temperatures must be comfortable so teachers can concentrate on teaching and kids can concentrate on learning. A few degrees can make a big difference in energy costs without sacrificing comfort. A rule of thumb is to consider setting the thermostats at sixty-eight degrees for heating and seventy-eight degrees for cooling. Custodians, teachers, and students can work together to solve the comfort issue by following a few basic principles. First, do not block the airflow around vents. Keep bookcases and other bulky

items away from heating and cooling units as they do not block and/or absorb the warm (or cool) air that should be coming into the classroom. Second, minimize the operating hours of heating and cooling systems. If a system isn't on, it isn't using energy. Third, turn down the heat in the hallways. Finally, save heat overnight. Limit after school activities to as few heating/cooling zones as possible so you can turn off systems in the rest of the building.

5. Stop leaks. At one school kids made translucent window quilts that, when hung on the interior, provided insulation and made a noticeable difference in classroom comfort. Also look at your faucets. For the price of a seventy-nine-cent washer you can save hundreds of dollars in lost water at a leaky faucet.

6. Turn off computers. It should come as no surprise that computers represent the fastest growing percentage of electricity consumption in schools today. Because monitors account for 80 percent of the energy used by a computer, students should turn off monitors that will not be used for the next class period. All computer equipment should be turned off at the end of the school day unless network technicians specifically instruct otherwise.

7. Don't let savings slip down the drain. Water conservation can fit nicely into the curriculum. At one elementary school, a teacher noticed that her first graders tended to run faucets for a long time when washing their hands. As part of their math class, the children measured how much water was wasted, put a timer on the sink, and checked to see how well they were practicing energy-efficient behavior. Teenagers at one high school traced the source of water supplied to the school and then tracked where it went after it left the school. The project integrated history, English, and mathematics. The students learned about the history of diseases spread by untreated water systems, industrial pollution of the water supply, and efforts to rectify the situation.

8. Recycle. Many schools undertake a recycling program for its educational benefit, for savings, and for revenue it can generate, particularly for paper, cardboard, and aluminum. Recycling and saving energy aren't just about cutting operating budgets. They are also about making kids aware of the energy they consume in their daily lives and how their consumption affects the environment. Kids take

that awareness home and share it with their families. Parents are reacting. "I'm not sure exactly what you are doing at school, but at home I keep walking into rooms where the lights, TV, and computer have been turned off after we leave the area."

Waste not, want not. Energy conservation is not for the faint of heart at one charter school in Portland, Oregon. There you will find a dumpster-sized worm bed, where 20,000 Georgia Red Wigglers are gobbling leftovers from the school lunch program. The worms are voracious. Almost as voracious as the conservation program that is saving the school money. The staff is changing old habits and teaching new values in ways that seem to please tree-huggers and bottom-liners alike.

Awareness strategies abound. Americorps volunteers are jumping into school dumpsters and showing kids how to search for recyclable materials that have been thrown away. Middle school students are recording energy consumption, making comparisons on spreadsheets, and recommending conservation strategies to the community. Kids are bringing home such water conservation ditties as, "If it's yellow, let it mellow, if it's brown, flush it down."

Throughout the country kids are learning. The physical building has lessons to teach. We are introducing the next generation to a conservation life style in terms of energy conservation.

Another area representative of the tangled web of finances surrounds managing construction costs. State legislators have been talking about taking a greater role in financing school construction, but so far this did not really translate into any concrete action or legislation. Currently forty states provide construction money to local districts. This does not include charter schools or alternative schools.

The most costly areas related to construction are the search for solutions, handicapped accessible bathrooms and ramps, and the required stainless steel kitchen.

How do you stay afloat when it comes to finances and school operation? The following statements explain how a once swamped school district reached sound financial ground.

This small school district found sound financial ground (sound as any school system can be today) by enduring sacrifice, improving business practices, encouraging entrepreneurialism, working for adequate state funding, improving community relations, and simply not spending one more penny than the district received.

The sacrifice. Salary freezes. Keep cuts as far away from the classroom as possible so as not to gut the educational program. Do not sacrifice student achievement. If a district is on the decline, parents will take their children elsewhere leaving you with what has come to be known as "bright flight." Therefore, continue to create high-quality programs even under severe financial constraints.

Saving (and making) money. Use business consultants to conduct a management study of the school's administration. You may need to reorganize central administration eliminating some positions and creating others. Develop and design programs that would be eligible for grant funding (school-to-work, technology, adult education, and a family literacy program). One successful program is a Grand Friends program that brings retirees into the schools as volunteers. Lobby for a change in the state funding formula.

Improve community relations. Work actively within the local community. Understand the needs of your community and seek to gain support for the school. Expand business partnerships. Commit to volunteerism by giving back to the community instead of only asking for help.

Market our schools. Use the media by networking with local radio and cable stations. Sell solutions not problems. Avoid controversy and get organized and remain in control. Remember, money matters.

Financial experts have arrived at fourteen ways schools can save money. Sure you could fire all the staff, but there are better ways to save money, ways that don't hurt student achievement, don't hurt staff, and don't bring screaming mobs to the boardroom.

If your district is looking for ways to save money, consider these ideas:

- Don't pay for what you and the district employees don't need. Personnel costs are the biggest expense in any district, and the cost of employee benefits often grows faster than the cost of salaries, even when some employees do not need or use all of the benefits. Many districts have found that requiring employers to pay a small premium for health insurance encourages employees already covered by a spouse's insurance to opt out of the district's plan. One school district has found another way to cut insurance costs—almost 120 employees have agreed to forgo their coverage, in exchange for checks amounting to 40 percent of the saved premium.

- Turn off lights. Utility bills are the second largest expense for most districts and the cost of lighting accounts for 40 percent of those utility bills. Changing how people use lights can turn a district's electric bill down up to 15 percent. The changes can be as simple as turning off lights in a hallway or dimming the security lights after midnight.
- Change light bulbs. You can cut your lighting costs by 50 percent if you have not done any retrofits in the past. Replace incandescent bulbs and old fluorescents with the new compact florescent lights, known as T-8s.
- Check your bills carefully. Mistakes happen. Getting refunds is no problem, but someone has to find out whether a refund is due. The utility is not going to find it for you. Checking bills also alerts you to other ways you can save money. Leaky toilets can flush away as much as $30,000 in water every year.
- Shop for better deals. Recent deregulation means both traditional and start-up companies are competing for utility contracts.
- Form (or join) a co-op. School districts are eligible for discounts on everything from crayons to telephone services.
- Keep track of what you own. Check, sell, and reduce excess inventory.
- Consider keeping schools open year-round. This also has a positive impact on student achievement too. Studies show that test scores do not go down in year-round schools.
- Be polite. Avoid lawsuits. Listen to complaints and make an attempt to solve the problem.
- Get along with administration and your superintendent or director. Buyouts are costly.
- Consider offering early retirement incentives. Many districts say they save money by offering early retirement incentives to experienced employees. The idea is that high-salaried people will leave and be replaced by lower-salaried people.
- Speed up construction on new buildings.
- Look for cheaper ways to collect taxes.
- Beware of false savings. Turning off the air exchangers in an effort to keep hot (or cold) air out of a school building can lead to problems with indoor air quality. Also, don't skimp on preventative mainte-

nance. Take computers as an example. Computer viruses can run rampant and fearless students can goof with the desktop. Now figure the cost of a staff member's time to straighten these things out, and spending $29 on a security package is money well spent. So how can you tell false savings from the real thing? Hire smart people who know ways to save money.

Managers help schools stay out of the red and avoid financial disaster. We have all heard of schools hitting rock bottom and declaring financial insolvency. How does such a financial disaster happen? What are the warning signals?

Financial disasters do not occur out of the blue. Case histories of failed schools report there had been plenty of warning signals—what are called the red flags of fiscal disaster. These are the signals of impending trouble:

- A pattern of overspending. The schools spend more money than is available in the general fund. They use short-term loans to cover operating expenses and lease equipment they can't afford to buy.
- To much optimism about their resources. The schools routinely overestimate how much money they should receive as interest income and from state and federal sources (special education, Title 1, Indian Education, etc.).
- Inadequate financial controls. The school boards don't have or don't update written procedures for submitting purchase orders, issuing checks, and reconciling accounts. Purchases are authorized when no money is available.
- A breakdown in basic business operations. Short-handed business offices do not keep up with accounts payable, so monthly budget reports and financial statements are often misleading. Financial reports to the state Department of Education and Finance are either late or incomplete. Many schools have no idea how much money they have on hand. There are no procedures for tracking their fiscal assets.
- Inattention to audits. Many schools ignore the auditor's recommendations.
- Out-of-control personnel practices. Many schools lack personnel position control. These schools hire people they thought they needed, even when the positions have not been included in the budget. Job

descriptions, if available, are out of date and the boards agree to salary increases beyond the state mandated cost-of-living adjustments, even when they have no designated revenue sources for the excess.
- Failure to plan ahead. The schools have no long-range financial plans, have no reserve funds for emergency or contingency purposes, and have deferred maintenance. They result in a cash flow management problem and no earmark of revenue for monthly bills.

Looking at schools that closed due to financial problems has resulted in a compelling list of do's and don'ts for current schools that want to stay in the black.

What to do:

- Do monitor adherence to board policy and administrative regulations, particularly as related to incurred debt, budget controls, and hiring practices. This means avoiding short-term debt. When you borrow against next year's income, you're mortgaging future operations and spending money you do not have.
- Do insist on an explicit rationale, along with budgeted revenue sources, for personnel raises that exceed your state's recommended cost-of-living adjustment.
- Do exercise caution in estimating average daily attendance (ADA). It is better to underestimate than to overestimate when you are counting on per-pupil revenue from state sources.
- Do insure that your school has a clear and adequate purchasing policy that requires more than one person to approve the expenditure of funds.
- Do insure that integrity of the budget as adopted in an open meeting is carried out as approved. The budget is a promise that you are making taxpayers, and many taxpayers see middle-of-the-year budget amendments as broken promises. You either have to say no to requests for extra money or be prepared to go public with an explanation of why you think the promise needs to be broken.
- Do monitor declining revenue closely and take necessary action to keep the budget in balance. Don't count on juggling the books to make things right in the last month of the fiscal year.

- Do reserve a certain percentage of your budget for unforeseen events—10 to 15 percent is an average amount.
- Do require administrators to develop a five- to ten-year financial plan that includes all known financial commitments. Make sure the plan is updated annually.
- Do enlist expert legal counsel in drawing up contracts for construction projects and for any leases the school may enter into.

What not to do:

- Don't approve personnel contracts that exceed resources allocated in the budget. Because employee expenses typically account for about 80 percent of a school's budget, it is important to know what you can afford before you agree to anything.
- Don't miss an opportunity to review audit recommendations and the administration's progress in implementation. Know the background and experience of your auditors.
- Don't ignore fiscal reports or balance sheets showing the financial position of your school. It is appropriate to request such reports on a regular monthly basis.
- Don't become complacent once things seem to be resolved. Continue oversight for a specific period of time or until you are confident procedures have become systematic.
- Don't let your own lack of familiarity with financial matters keep your school board from exercising its proper role as financial stewards. The best of intentions—improving student achievement, creating better community relations, improving the moral climate of the school—cannot be achieved without taking care of the school's financial business first. Learn how to read financial statements, how to ask intelligent questions about school finance, where to seek financial advice, and how to spot the red flags of fiscal disaster.

It is not often that we have an opportunity to look at the financials in a positive light. It is not often that we have an opportunity to encourage children to act locally while thinking globally. Remember, kids care, often passionately, about the environment, so let's seize this opportunity to create energy-conservation programs that turn passion into memorable lessons with the school building itself serving as a laboratory and the financial benefits going to the school's bottom line. Managers care about construction costs and avoiding financial disaster and they know how to keep an eye on the needs of the school. With persistence we can work together to untangle this tangled web of finances.

5

Accountability

If you do what you've always done, you'll get what you've always gotten.

—Anonymous

Across the country a single idea has become the new educational reform—accountability. Politicians are for it, superintendents and school managers and leaders are doing it, and parents and concerned community members say that more of it will improve our schools. Accountability suggests a responsiveness that people do not regularly experience in their interactions with most large institutions. Parents want quality education and they want attention to their children's needs. When concerns are raised, these parents want constructive responses, and when responses are lacking, they want access to decision makers able to address their concerns. Accountability is ultimately a value. It is developed through relationships. It must be a motivating force that guides daily practice within a school. Accountability also requires clear, measurable goals. Being accountable, knowing that the doors stay open only if students succeed, gives urgency to a school's mission. Accountability is a matter of taking responsibility for the content and process of goals set, decisions made, actions taken, and outcomes that result from them. It is about making agreements and engaging in activities with the full expectation that they must be carried out in the most competent, high-quality, conscientious manner possible.

Parents say: "I want my child's school to be safe, to teach the basics along with teaching respect for authority, and I want to see proof that this is being done." Others say: "I like that my school is accountable, even with unconventional, creative approaches toward teaching." Both views are important for student achievement. If schools can't do a better job of educating all students, parents will get out of public education altogether.

When school officials vow to resign or take pay cuts if student's test scores don't rise, you can be sure that the age of accountability is here.

The challenge is simple, if daunting: to make enormous improvements in quality and time to task, and at the same time, greatly reduce costs. The economic facts of life have dramatically changed in recent decades and the facts of American education have not kept pace. Since 1950 the proportion of American jobs available to people with limited literacy has been steadily decreasing, and the proportion requiring advanced education has swiftly risen. Despite a slow, steady rise in the educational achievements of our high school graduates as evidenced by the rising numbers attending college, the National Center on Educational Statistics reports that half or more students without a diploma have no more than an eighth grade level of literacy. This is well below what it will take to land jobs that enable wage earners to support a family above poverty level.

The only way a school can survive is by learning *how* to educate virtually all of their students to a much higher standard at a cost no greater than current costs. That is why coming up with an adequate response to this challenge is no fad. It is a matter of survival.

In the past, when educators have talked about accountability, they have asked, "How can we produce public data on performance?" But the public has been asking a different question: "If students are not performing, who is responsible and what should happen to them?" The public is fed up with excuses, demanding improved student performance at no increase in cost. Public educators do themselves no good by complaining. Whether we call it accountability to the public (as educators would have it), the challenge is to get much better results at no increase in cost.

School reform efforts over the past twenty years have helped pave the way for accountability measures. The first such reform is site-based management, which responds to the call for pushing decisions about how to get the job done right, and holding the people making the product or rendering the service accountable. In this model the faculty of the school is able to make the important decisions about how the needs of the students could best be met, within the bounds determined by the standards set by the larger system. Whatever rewards come from doing a good job would be shared among the faculty, and the faculty would suffer whatever consequence came from poor performance.

Merit pay for teachers is the second precursor to modern accountability. Following the release of the famous federal report, *A Nation at Risk*, in 1983, many states decided to "get tough" on teachers and insist that their pay be related to the quality of their teaching. Tennessee took the lead in that direction and many other states followed.

Teachers, however, hated this system and in the end, successfully mobilized political power to defeat it. Teachers everywhere had seen principals using their power to reward those they believe to be loyal and punish those they believe to be disloyal. The merit pay plans typically relied on principals to make the decision as to whose teaching was meritorious.

The third development that laid the groundwork for the new accountability was the move toward academic standards. From former president Bush's call to governors to join him at the nation's first educational summit in 1989 to President Clinton's call for national, but not federal standards, at the beginning of his second term, an enormous amount of work has been devoted to teaching in core disciplines.

Three models of accountability: Kentucky, Chicago, and Edmonton in the province of Alberta, Canada, can help us focus on the student and his/her success in school.

The landmark Kentucky Educational Reform Act of 1990 established a six-part "accountability index." Every two years, student progress has been measured by statewide test scores in reading, mathematics, social studies, and science, as well as writing performance on open-ended test questions. A problem-solving activity and portfolios of children's work is also included. An additional score has been factored in that measures attendance and graduating rates. In this system the schools have essentially competed not against each other but against their own record trying to do better each year than they did in the previous year. Rewards are given on the basis of the scores the students received.

If rewards are one side of the accountability coin, penalties are the flip side. In Chicago, 1995 reforms brought schools under the direct control of Democratic mayor Richard Daley. More than one hundred schools were placed on probation and were required to get help from one of a number of providers of outside technical assistance.

The drive for accountability has not been simply a story of standards, assessment, empowerment, and rewards/consequences. Holding people accountable also requires being clear about who is responsible for what. That is the centerpiece of the Edmonton system, which has revolutionized relations between schools and the central educational office.

Edmonton's pioneering system means streamlining the organizational "boss." It then allocates district resources in dollars to the schools each of which will be held responsible and accountable for student results. Poor performance results in no dollars.

In all three cases, Kentucky, Chicago, and Edmonton, control of the program and budget moved to the schools. Rewards were given for good results. Consequences were given if results were poor.

A comprehensive accountability model requires the following functions of individual schools:

- Choose a leadership team for the school to develop and implement the school's goals and objectives.
- Decide on a code of behavior to establish order and discipline.
- Add your own standards and goals.
- Decide on the measures to be used to assess progress toward the goals and the methods to be used to track progress.
- Decide on the best structure to implement the program.
- Decide what skills and knowledge the staff will need to execute the program and what professional development program best provides for the skills and knowledge inclusion.
- Decide how the school wants to involve parents, social services, public health agencies, local employers, and other cultural staff.
- Implement the plan and revise it continuously based on analysis of the data on student performance.
- Provide all the information required.

It is no secret that accountability is a challenge. Schools are different. Look at charter schools. These schools are typically thinly administered and free from many of the operational, financial, and educational constraints that hamstring conventional public schools. In exchange for this freedom from constraints, charter schools are accountable for results. But in creating an accountability system to monitor their programs and progress toward achieving results, they find themselves facing several challenges.

If the accountability system created to monitor progress to results is too onerous, it may deflect the school leadership from the pursuit of sound teaching and learning. If it is too prescriptive, forcing everything into the familiar categories of conventional schools, it may constrain the school's ability to do things differently. If it is too superficial it may not yield the requisite information. If too laid back, it may not detect serious trouble in time to take appropriate action. And if it is too flexible in allowing each school to define its own terms, it may provide no basis for needed comparisons.

There are three challenges that charter schools and other nontraditional schools face as they negotiate the shoals of school accountability.

First, in grappling with school accountability, it is essential for managers and leaders to keep in mind the distinction between the ends of education and the means used to achieve them. The standards imply the ends of education—what we expect our young people to know and to do so that they are prepared for responsibility in living in the world of work, family, and citizenship. The means concern the ways our schools are organized and the methods they employ to assist our young people in acquiring knowledge and skills.

A second challenge concerns state testing systems and "fit" between what a school says it will do and what a state testing system constricts it from doing. For example, standardized testing programs used by states and communities for conventional school account purposes may not suit a charter school's distinctive mission or philosophy (or its student body, especially if it enrolls many at-risk youth). The standards built into such tests may be unrealistically high for one student population and absurdly low for another. The grade level assumptions of the tests may not correspond to the school's scope and sequence. Conversely, a school's use of innovative assessment techniques and indicators whose reliability is not proven, or whose results are not comparable, may cause doubts about the school's reported success. In simplest terms, what a school was founded to teach may not be exactly what the state or district measures. The ways in which the school most desires to demonstrate its effectiveness may not yield the kinds of information that the community seeks from schools.

A final challenge concerns the two "agents" to which a charter school is accountable. Every charter school is accountable to a "higher authority"—the charter sponsor. But it is also accountable to its customers via the marketplace. Dissatisfied customers—parents and teachers—can vote with their feet and flee. The school, in other words, can be abandoned by those who attend (or work) in it if the school is not a satisfactory place in which to study or work.

Without timely and reliable information on student and school performance, accountability will not work, whether for policymakers or for the educational marketplace, particularly parents. Good information is the starting point for making good decisions. Strive for a fair, balanced, and realistic judgment.

Accountability can make or break an educational reform movement. It will be the primary source of evidence as to whether the movement is making a valuable contribution to the improved education of American children and the renewal of United States public education or is another half-tried reform fad that sinks into the sand like so many others.

If you want your fledgling charter school to survive and flourish make sure the manager and leader are accountable for their school's success. The accountability issue, more than any other, will make or break the charter movement.

For charter schools, accountability is the key to fending off criticism and staying alive. Establishing goals for students, teachers, and parents and maintaining fiscal responsibility are among the key elements of success to charter schools. These elements will break down resistance to charter schools from the community and those within the school system.

Let's look further at charter schools through a report card on charter school accountability.

In 1988, when maverick American Federation of Teachers president Albert Shanker came up with the idea of charter schools, he envisioned publicly funded but independent laboratory schools that would strike a bargain with the system; less red tape in exchange for more achievement, innovation, and accountability.

However, on the tenth anniversary of the experiment launch (July 2000), there is highly critical assessment of the movement that now claims 2119 schools and more than a half million students in thirty-seven states and the District of Columbia (Cawell, *Newsweek* 2002). While some distinctive new schools have been established, the report concludes that, too often, charter schools have not lived up to their end of the bargain. They have not been accountable. Charters spend more on administration and less on instruction than local public schools. Student performance is usually no better and often worse than traditional district schools. The study found that few charters are doing anything truly innovative.

"We wanted charters to be incubators of reform and we supported many that were," says current AFT president, Sandra Feldman (Cawell, *Newsweek* 2002). "But as we look across the country now, it is quite disappointing that so many have not lived up to their promises." Feldman says the union remains committed to ensuring charters succeed, but says that will only happen if states pass tough new accountability laws, or enforce the ones they already have.

Traditional public schools can take lessons from charter schools on accountability. In addition to academic goals for achievement, charter schools often write into their charters certain specific goals and programs of their own devising, activities that are central to their own self-concepts and missions. (Heart of the Earth Center for American Indian Education Charter School, a K–12 program in Minneapolis, Minnesota, requires twelve years of cultural classes including Ojibwe and Lakota languages, American Indian history and tradition, and drum, dance, and native art.)

Programs vary widely depending on the school's philosophy, its target clientele, the needs of the community, and so forth. Some are curricular, shaping what the school teaches and how it accomplishes this. Boston's City on a Hill Charter School has a special goal that requires comprehensive civic education and community involvement for each student. Curricular goals may also focus on a discipline (math, science, and foreign languages) or the development of special skills (performing or theater arts, video editing and production, and music).

Other charter school goals may involve special categories of students (the disabled or those in the juvenile justice system) or the parents of children at a school. For example, California's Fenton Avenue Charter School has a goal that involves maintaining a parent education center that conducts continuing education programs for students' parents, including English as a Second Language and citizenship programs. Some charter school goals are student specific, aiming to increase attendance and graduation rates, decrease dropout rates, and reduce disciplinary actions.

Still other goals combine elements of a school's life (curriculum, parent involvement, or community involvement). In Franklin, Massachusetts, the parent-founded Benjamin Franklin Classical Charter School has created a goal that entails a parent involvement program that is integrated with the core knowledge curriculum of the school and linked with a student character education program. It includes using parents as teachers' aides, mentors, and role models. Homework activities involving parents are assigned that support the school's character education program.

As stated earlier, many charter schools have accountability compacts. The following lists some areas for which organizational and operational goals may be set for inclusion in the compact. The following goals are viable for all schools:

- Make a provision for families to be active participants in their children's education and in the school's operation.
- Develop plans for working relationships and service links with community organizations.
- Support the organization and culture of the school and the degree to which both organization and culture promote student achievement, learning, and responsible citizenship.
- Institute policies, practices, and programs likely to make the school a safe and orderly environment for learning.
- Make provisions for professional development of teachers, administrators, and other school staff.
- Devise a planning process that ensures that the interests of the community, parents, teachers, and other stakeholders are represented.
- Build a stable, effective governance model that is capable of providing strong vision and continuity of leadership and management.
- Employ people possessing the professional (leadership and management) skills needed for organizational, financial, pedagogical, legal, and other tasks required to operate a well-functioning school.

In short, an accountability plan should provide the school director, the school community, and the general public with a set of goals and indicators that will help them determine whether a school is meeting its nonacademic organizational responsibilities.

States raise the bar and are accountable for results. Standards-based reform is not a panacea. We know from our work in the classroom that we ask too little of all American students. That lack of rigor is ten times worse in high poverty schools, Without clear guidance about which work is good enough, schools inevitably settle for low expectations for poverty-level children. Without a clear sense of what you want students to do, you run the risk of heading off in the wrong directions.

What is involved in putting standards in place?

- A school must develop standards in core subject areas using various state and national standards as its guide.
- Involve parents, students, teachers, and community members in the process. This kind of involvement gives ownership to everybody.
- Give information to teachers, parents, and students.
- Invest in training.
- Invest in resources.
- Align the curriculum with the standards.
- Commitment.

As we look at development we look at hurdles and challenges. We must address the following:

- Resistance to change (it is easier to maintain the existing system)
- Cost
- Data measurement and interpretation
- Teacher training
- Finding the time for professional development
- Maintaining focus on the students at the bottom of the ladder
- Addressing the issue that ranking schools by test scores does nothing to improve the quality of education

Accountability is strengthened by listening to the public and the community. Empower the community by holding conversations that involve listening and learning. In other words, dialogue does not allow a monologue to happen. Create a community-wide dialogue, not a school-initiated monologue. Create parent teams to assist.

Listen as you look at the curriculum. If we want to keep the learning fresh, we have to make it possible for our students to go from outside the subject to inside.

Listen to the teachers. Teaching should be a continuing expedition of self-discovery, from growing toward the profession as a student to growing toward the profession as a practitioner. Sharing your enthusiasm about the subject you are teaching will help you be accountable to your students.

A huge piece of the accountability pie in all schools is getting ready for the federal- and state-mandated standardized tests.

Select the answer that best completes the following statement. Standardized tests:

a. Have been used by educators for generations
b. Are controversial topics in schools today
c. Sometimes cause undo misery in teachers and students
d. All of the above

If you answered (d) you are correct.

The question is, how can you effectively support our test-taking student? One way is to put the tests in perspective. According to Darcy Ann Olson, Director of Education and Child Policy at the Cato Institute, parents should not take an active role in "preparing" students for standardized tests unless high test anxiety is a problem for the student (Wolk 2001). However, most parents may want to call the school prior to the test and find out where the student will test or any other bit of information that will help the student understand the setting ahead of time.

Olson also suggests that parents explore web sites of private educational services such as Sylvan Learning Centers, which offers countless tips on how to sharpen test-taking skills and how to help prepare students for the types of questions found on standardized tests. Educational services may also have take-home tests that parents can give to determine what skills students have mastered.

Another way to lessen anxiety is to encourage good study habits throughout the entire school year. You can't cram for these once-a-year standardized tests. Leaders and managers must emphasize and provide realistic appraisals about the standardized tests. The test may be important but doing poorly on tests is not the end of the world.

Catching poor readers before they fail is a crucial issue. Poor readers can be identified as early as age five by testing the child's ability to rapidly name numbers, letters, and letter sounds. The sooner a child can receive effective and intensive instruction in his or her reading and math the better chance this child has to be successful in school.

Look for a reading program that includes:

- Recognition that students must understand that words are made up of different sounds. They can then associate sounds with written words and read groups of words.
- Students who have trouble learning to read need to be specifically taught the relationships of letters, words, and sounds.
- Each child needs a different amount of reading practice.
- Phonics instruction should be taught as part of a comprehensive literature-based reading program.

Many parents and community members are concerned about making standards work. First, however, we need to define standards. High and rigorous academic standards are:

- A way to establish what all students need to know and be able to accomplish
- A result of a public and political outcry for increased accountability in schools
- Not yet well implemented in most schools, although not for want of trying (Maybe we need to go a step further and follow Yoda's advice in *The Empire Strikes Back*. Yoda says, "Try? There is no try. There is only do or do not do.")
- Fraught with challenges and difficulties, but still an opportunity to raise the achievement of all students
- A bipartisan reform that offers a common ground on which advocates of good education can unite

Teaching a common body of essential skills and knowledge need not narrow the curriculum or inhibit good teaching practice. The more we expect from students, the more they will achieve. I think we need to look at standards as here today, here tomorrow.

Most parents and educators believe that state tests help identify students who need extra attention, make students pay more attention, and help to hold schools accountable for raising achievement. The key lies in the execution, the translation of the broad areas upon which we agree into policies and practices that play out in the classrooms.

When standards are well devised and implemented and have accountability provisions tied to them, the nature of teaching and learning can change. Standards can lead to a richer more challenging curriculum. They can foster conversation and collaboration among teachers within and across schools. They can create a more productive dialogue among teachers and parents. They can also help focus everyone's attention on raising student achievement. The public will continue to support standards so long as the students who reach them are prepared to succeed in the next grade, in college, and in meaningful careers.

Program evaluation is difficult, controversial, and an integral part of accountability. A lot of people want to know what is going on inside schools today. Parents want to know what their children are studying and how they are doing. House-hunting families looking at schools want to know what percentage of students go on to a four-year college and how their students score on SATs. Curriculum committees want to know how pilot projects are working before they decide whether to expand the programs. Taxpayers want to know why test scores are going down while expenditures are going up. Managers want to know all of these things in order to restructure school programs.

Despite the continuing interest in accountability and improvement, schools are notoriously weak in program evaluation. Program evaluation is generally ignored because it is difficult, controversial, and expensive. Effective assessment is a rigorous task that requires smart, creative people willing to work hard on something that is often not popular. To many people working in schools, the evaluation process seems to threaten their careers while it puts money in the pockets of professional consultants and takes teachers away from their classrooms. But when it is done right, program evaluation can lead to dramatic improvements in instruction, curriculum, and student achievement.

The following are tips for program evaluation success:

- Focus on the question, "Are the students learning?"
- Accept the challenge. Designing and implementing evaluation systems is by nature both art and science. On one hand, creativity is needed to develop imaginative ways of measuring qualitative factors; on the other hand, the overall evaluation process needs to be systematic.

- Commit your resources. Program evaluation is expensive. Training needs to happen.
- Identify specific programs and their cost.
- Let people know what you are doing. Education is scary to many people. Teachers feel uncomfortable with evaluators visiting their classrooms and administrators worry that their jobs are on the line.
- Be efficient. Evaluation is hard work. Working sessions should be facilitated with refreshments, comfortable surroundings, and other necessities. Don't waste people's valuable time.
- Evaluate the evaluation. Examine its costs and how well it is being done.

The approach to accountability should be primarily results-driven, not resource- or input- or rule-driven.

The purpose of a results-driven accountability plan is to gather information that will help the school community, district and state authorities, and the general public to know whether the school is reaching its goals. The plan should be designed to provide information needed to measure and track the school's progress toward its goals, make program adjustments when needed, and report to the parents, community, and authorities on performance and progress.

The accountability plan is the mechanism through which the school indicates the goals (outcomes) and performance levels it elects to be held accountable for attaining. However, it is important to recognize that the performance will be compared by the public and the media to that of other public schools.

Begin with a clear description and understanding of the mission of your school. Peter Drucker (2001, 1, 3) emphasizes this point: "The mission comes first. . . . [A]nd the first job of the leader is to think through and define the mission of the institution. For example, a school that is a magnet for math and science students will have a different mission than one for youth involved in the juvenile justice system.

There are four general criteria for holding schools accountable:

1. The school must produce satisfactory academic progress by its students on state- or district-wide tests and similar measures.
2. Demonstrate success in meeting nonacademic goals, including those that are unique to the school's mission and design.

3. The school must provide evidence that it is a viable organization, that it is using public funds responsibly and complying with management and governance issues.
4. The school must comply with applicable laws and regulations.

A school must set academic goals for itself. These goals should be based on the school's mission and respond to the educational needs of the student population the school is serving. One example of an academic goal for an elementary school is to provide all students with a rich and challenging curriculum. An academic goal for a high school is to develop in students the knowledge and skills needed for success in college or employment after graduation.

Goals need to be set in terms of standards, content, and performance. Content standards define the knowledge and skills that students should acquire at various stages of their education. Performance standards spell out the expected levels of proficiency (what is good enough to advance from one stage to the next).

An example of a content standard in math might be: by the end of eighth grade each student can do multidigit multiplication problems. A performance standard would be: given ten multiplication problems using multidigits, each student can compute the correct answer for eight of these ten problems in less than fifteen minutes.

Standards should address core academic areas, be at least as rigorous as those of other countries, be measurable so students can demonstrate whether they have attained and mastered the standards, and be balanced and cumulative. Standards should define both knowledge and skills and build upon each other.

Test measurements are the mechanisms that schools use to gauge whether students are learning to the standards set for them. Different assessments should include norm- or criterion-referenced tests, essay-style questions, use of portfolios, student self-reports, exhibitions, and teacher observations. Collecting baseline achievement data is important to the process. Standards, testing, and consequences are three critical pieces for all schools. By focusing on performance, schools are able to unite the interests of their school community and build the necessary trust and confidence to continue doing what is best for the students.

Accountability. Is it a buzzword or a reform movement? You be the judge.

6

Who's in Our Classrooms?

It is a great satisfaction knowing that for a brief point in time you made a difference.

—Irene Natividad, Philippine-American political activist

When children grow up in the worst circumstances and yet thrive, the difference isn't the circumstance of their chaotic home life, but it is often the fact that one caring adult really is involved in their lives. Often that one caring adult is a teacher. Students work harder, achieve more, and attribute more importance to schoolwork in classrooms in which they feel liked, accepted, and respected by their teacher.

Too often classroom management systems built on trust and support in the early grades are replaced with compliance and obedience in the later grades. Instilling positive feelings in students will not result from pep talks or positive self-image lectures, but rather, from planned learning experiences. A teacher must structure opportunities into each child's daily routine that will enable him or her to experience feelings of competence, belonging, usefulness, potency, and optimism.

In an ideal classroom environment, teachers support a child's desire to find out about things. Classrooms are filled with books, magazines, tapes, computers, art supplies, and science equipment. Resources abound. If we want to prepare our students for the future, we cannot continue to teach as we did in the past. Modern technology, curriculum and innovative methods will help move us into the future and at the same time help us explore the past if the questions arise. A good teacher tells a student what is out there to learn, shows an enthusiasm for acquiring knowledge for the purpose of understanding, and then turns the student loose to learn at his/her own pace.

It is the responsibility of the management and administration force in the school to build a better teacher. A good teacher is the single best thing you can give the kids in your school. The trouble is, it is not always easy to find a good teacher. Teachers need to know how to teach and they need to know how students learn.

I have found that there are five necessities with respect to quality teachers:

1. Teachers are committed to students and their learning.
2. Teachers know their subjects and how to teach them.
3. Teachers are responsible for managing and monitoring student learning.
4. Teachers think systematically about their practice and learn from experience.
5. Teachers are members of learning communities.

As Henry Brooks Adams said in 1907, "A teacher affects eternity. He can never tell where his influence stops." Politicians and the general public are increasingly vocal about the power of a good teacher. More and more people are realizing that teachers are an influential force in the lives of students. In our present society a teacher may spend more time with a student than the student's family.

Research has determined three indicators of teacher quality that account for improved student achievement in core subject areas. These indicators include classroom practices, professional development, and the teacher's educational level and experience.

Many educators believe it takes from five to eight years to develop teaching expertise. If new teachers, regardless of their qualifications on entry, are to make a difference in students' lives, they will need incentives, respectable salaries, and appreciation. Even more, they will need professional support.

What does it take to be a good teacher? I want teachers to have depth and breadth of knowledge and understanding in their disciplines, the essential questions and concepts as well as the content, and a command of the specific subjects they are assigned to teach.

I want teachers who have a rich repertoire of methods and materials, and who know how to tap into this repertoire to make topics they teach fascinating for kids. I want teachers to be creative and passionate. I want teachers to craft their teaching so to consider their own classrooms as laboratories for improving teaching and learning. As teachers use the research others have done and conduct their own research, they can better redefine for themselves what it means to be a teacher.

Improving the quality of the teaching force is essential. We need to look at the characteristics of expert teachers, ask ourselves if certified teachers are better, and challenge ourselves to attract more highly qualified teachers. It takes five to eight years to master the craft of teaching. Only through experiencing the complexity of the classroom does a teacher learn. A college degree in education only takes you so far. It prepares you to be a beginner in a complex world.

Expert teachers have case knowledge. They can go back in their memory banks to compare situations and figure out what to do. When expert teachers encounter a new student, a new learning problem, or new curriculum materials, they have references stored in memory banks. Expert teachers are also much better at capturing teachable moments. They know what is going on in the classroom at the time. They know how to get the class from point A to point B. Novices have no such experiences stored in their memory banks. Of course, some novices never get a clue about what is going on; they never learn from experience.

Professional education gives teachers more familiarity with cultural, academic, and human diversity. Methods courses teach the pedagogical side of education. Without a professional knowledge base, a teacher takes a lot longer to understand how students learn and what and how they need to be taught. Imagine going into a hardware store and not knowing the names of the things you need to buy. Professional education teaches the vocabulary of schools (learning disabled, gifted, mean, median, mode). And it teaches the pedagogy. What does it mean to do reciprocal teaching? How does one teach math in a way that allows kids to discover the answers? Untrained teachers cannot invent reciprocal teaching on their own. Learning some tips about classroom management during a short-term summer program is not enough.

So in light of these issues, why do new teachers choose to teach?

Far from feeling indifferent or disgruntled, new teachers say they believe in what they do, care about their students, and are deeply committed to their profession.

Given the high priority of education in recent years and its centrality on the agenda of the Bush administration, a national discussion of standards, accountability, and high-stakes testing is sure to be front and center. Whatever the outcome, as states and school districts debate issues, classroom teachers will inevitably be on the firing line. Our dependence on teachers to deliver the goods, to instruct, guide, inspire, motivate, cajole, and occasionally produce learning in our kids is irrefutable; and unfortunately, our scrutiny of these teachers will only intensify if students continue to fail academically.

Assumptions and hypothesis about teachers—how much they know, how much they care, and how well prepared they are—are behind some policy initiatives intended to ratchet up student performance. Teacher pay and licensing, tenure and accountability, and teaching methods and morale have joined a long list of contentious issues encircling public education.

In the book *A Sense of Calling: Who Teaches and Why?*, Farkas, Johnson, and Foleno focus on what new teachers (defined as those with five years experience or less) say about why they entered the teaching profession and what they think after they have been on the job. The book also captures the observations and concerns of those who hire and supervise teachers (school superintendents, principals, and directors) in communities across the United States and the prospects of young college students who did not choose teaching as a career. Many issues are probed in the book: Do new teachers entering the profession lack motivation and spirit, or do they bring energy and commitment with them? Have young people turned their backs on the profession? What would motivate young college graduates to take a second look at teaching as a career? Is money the chief obstacle to recruiting the most talented graduates? As a principal who hires teachers, I find myself wondering about motivation and spirit, as well as their sincerity for teaching. I always ask why the prospective candidate entered the teaching field.

Observers of the teaching profession and some of my colleagues differ on whether teacher quality is really declining. Some say that difficult working conditions and relatively low pay discourage talented young people from entering teaching. Some say that teacher quality has eroded as an unintended consequence of increased opportunities for women. Some fear that teaching now appeals to too many young people who have lackluster skills and little drive and who are lured by the promise of secure jobs with summers off and predictable pay raises. Adding any of these arguments together brings out broad fears that new teachers are routinely disgruntled and disaffected in a job that all agree requires latent judgment, enthusiasm, and skill.

An in-depth survey of 664 public school teachers and 250 private school teachers who have been in the classroom five years or less suggests a dramatically different picture (Berliner 2001). At least by their own report and that of administrators, most young teachers are highly motivated professionals who bring a strong sense of commitment and high morals to their work. New teachers see themselves as talented, hardworking professionals who have responded to a calling. They convey love of and a dedication to their craft.

New teachers are quick to point out that theirs is a profession that requires a sense of mission. More than eight in ten (86 percent) believe that only those with "a true sense of calling" should pursue the work. Most teachers feel enthusiasm for the job is a prerequisite for success. "If I am not excited about what I am doing, neither are the students. You have to sell it first. It is a package deal" (Boser 2000).

Many experts and decision makers voice concern that new teachers are overwhelmed when they first come into the profession and soon become frustrated and eager to leave. An analysis of a United States Department of Education study in *Education Week* (Boser 2000) concluded that about 20 percent of new teachers leave after a few years. Research by Berliner (2001) also shows a comparable number (19 percent) who predict that they will probably change careers.

Managers are trying to reform education by developing mentoring programs for teachers. Mentoring programs are important for two reasons. First they cut the dropout rate of teachers from roughly 50 percent to 15 percent during the first five years of teaching. The second reason that we need mentoring is a moral, rather than a pragmatic, one. We must not abandon beginners who have been placed in the complex world of teaching. Mentoring helps new teachers think about their experience and it helps them handle the emotional side of teaching. We find that teaching is an emotionally draining occupation. Teachers get caught up in the lives of the kids and their parents. New teachers need to know what a healthy response is and when to put up boundaries. They need clear advice about how to do something better or different the next time they teach it.

What the Department of Education report also shows, and what often seems lost in the debate over teacher retention, is a remarkable commitment, enthusiasm, and vitality of the majority who choose to stay in teaching. Many new teachers see their work as the commitment of a lifetime. Three-quarters say that they view their current profession as a "lifelong choice."

Most teachers are there by design, not by accident. Fifty-two percent say that it is something they had been hoping to do for some time; 34 percent say that they chose a teaching career in college. Some say they have been committed to teaching for so long that they can't remember thinking of doing anything else.

Once in the classroom, new teachers feel confident that they are in the right place. Ninety-one percent think that their skills and interests fit well with the demands of the profession. The overwhelming majority (80 percent) says that even if they were starting all over, they would opt to become teachers.

School administrators say that teachers are better than ever. It may not be all that surprising to hear new teachers describe themselves in positive terms, but what do their bosses—school superintendents and principals— think about the new crop of teachers? Farkas, Johnson, and Foleno (2000) randomly surveyed 511 public school principals and superintendents, asking them to pinpoint, through a full complement of questions, the strengths and weaknesses of new teachers, the areas where teacher supply is a problem, and the proposals to improve teacher quality that show the most promise. Overall, school administrators are remarkably upbeat. Almost all (98 percent) see the new teaching corps as highly motivated and energetic. One superintendent in an upstate New York school district said, "Two things motivate today's new teacher: Some teachers say that it is because they inspire their students, and they also say they think they can make a difference in students' lives" (Farkas, Johnson, and Foleno 2000).

It is obvious that many ingredients are necessary for teachers to thrive and be effective. Desire and motivation are only part of the equation. Knowledge, training, resources, and workplace conditions are key as well.

But what the Farkas, Johnson, and Foleno study told us is that, by their own account, beginning teachers are there because they want to be. They want to teach. The strength and vibrancy of their morale and motivation are noteworthy, if only because they strongly challenge a persistent assumption of the debate on teacher quality—that teachers lack motivation and spirit.

We have heard how teachers rate themselves (they feel confident, motivated, and ambitious) and now let's see what the students think. Students in several Minnesota charter schools developed the following questions when asked to rate teachers they knew:

- Does the teacher's approach to discipline help or hinder the learning atmosphere?
- Does the teacher use his or her time effectively?
- Does the teacher respect students like he or she would respect adults?
- Do students feel comfortable asking questions?
- Is the teacher sensitive to student interests and needs?
- Does what the teacher says get through to the students?
- Are the students actively interested?

Our students have a right to have answers to these questions. Learning is only possible when children look hopefully and joyfully to the future.

Teachers, in turn, respond that a significant part of student development comes through dialogue, reflecting on experience and looking at how our behavior affects others. If we do not know one another, we may not hear one another.

Next, let us ask the parents. Based on my experience as an administrator, the following are general questions that parents have asked about teachers:

- Does the teacher appear to enjoy teaching and believe in what he or she does in school?
- Does the teacher set high expectations and help students reach them?
- Does the teacher know the subject matter of the class and how to teach it?
- Does the teacher create a safe classroom where children are encouraged to pay attention, participate in class, and learn?
- Does the teacher deal with behavior problems fairly and consistently?

- Does the teacher define clearly what the child is to learn?
- Will the teacher call home? Teacher-to-parent contact through monthly phone calls strengthens the ties between school and home, leading to solid academic progress for many. Monthly phone calls also indicate to the parents that there is an additional level of caring on the teacher's behalf.

Parents ask about their children:

- Does the teacher treat my child fairly and with respect?
- Does the teacher contact me (parent) with any concerns about behavior or academics?

Parents ask about communicating:

- Does the teacher communicate or provide clear information about class expectations?
- Does the teacher use a variety of communication tools to report student progress?
- Is my child's teacher accessible and responsive?

Most educators enter the profession because they want to work with children, not because they want to work with children's parents. But getting along with parents is an inevitable part of any educator's job. We must understand parents' concerns, build parent support, and build and develop healthy school climates. Greater understanding leads to better communication. Teachers learn to interpret parents' behavior and manage to defuse volatile situations. Along this line of thought, good problem solvers are like good parents and spouses. All demonstrate patience, discipline, creativity, continuous improvement, repetition, honesty, and continuous learning.

Parents as partners in classrooms and schools is hardly a novel concept, but implementing the idea is far from easy. Parents and educators are not seeing eye to eye. Misunderstandings are rife and efforts to reform schools are stifled. Engagement means sitting at the table, not being pawns manipulated after decisions are made. Listen to people first, talk later.

The following are strategies to help turn parents from critics to allies:

- Dust off and roll out the welcome mat.
- Advertise your expertise.
- Implement an early warning system.
- Describe to parents familiar, positive portraits of their child.
- Convey shared values.
- Reassure parents that you will create a safe and protected environment for their child within the school.
- Empathize with parents that they indeed have a tough job.
- Be an effective and fair disciplinarian.
- Be a consistent role model.

In order to help develop teachers into the best they can be we need to attract a special group of people and encourage them to enter the teaching field. To do this, managers suggest removing the barriers for teacher candidates. Let's look at what Florida did to help alleviate their teacher shortage. In January 2001, a familiar headline appeared in the *Miami Herald*: "Florida Teacher Shortage Rings Schools' Alarm Bells, Educators' Stress, Low Pay Cited." The article began with a chilling image. Teachers across much of Florida are fleeing public schools in increasing numbers, saying they can no longer tolerate the stress, overcrowded classrooms, and low pay (Ferrechio and Grotto 2001).

Although the shortages in Florida are worse than in most states, the article tells a story that is national in scope. In countless newspaper articles, teachers cite poor working conditions, lack of support, bureaucracy, weak financial incentives, and growing job demands as reasons for leaving the classroom. Among new teachers, those who enter with little teacher education and those who receive little mentoring leave the most quickly, overwhelmed by complexities that they are poorly armed to meet. Noncompetitive salaries and inadequate incentives add to recruitment and retention problems. What would it take to produce the hoped-for headline, "Teachers Flocking to Public Schools: Improved Working Conditions, Better Incentives Cited"? The uphill climb to staff U. S. schools with qualified teachers is made that much steeper when new teachers leave in large numbers.

Policymakers can develop proactive strategies that do not trade student learning for haphazard teacher hiring. By designing a thoughtfully constructed package of professional standards, incentives, and improved working conditions, states will attract and keep more highly qualified teachers. Students will benefit, and the teaching profession will be more highly regarded for the important work that it does. What a wonderful front-page story that would make.

The traditional routes to teacher certification may deter potentially gifted teachers from entering the classroom. Streamlined alternative certification programs, teacher compensation plans, and school-level accountability may help open the door.

When Bill Babcock, an engineer with a graduate business degree, retired in 1993, he expected to spend most of his time fishing in Ormond Beach, Florida. But retirement on the beach proved too quiet. At his wife's suggestion he found his calling at a local middle school. In the spring of 2000, Babcock was named teacher of the year in Volusia County, Florida (Keller 2000). But if it had not been for an observant principal, a savvy district manager, and Babcock's perseverance, the students of Ormond Middle School might never have had this outstanding math instructor.

Babcock began by volunteering as an aide in computer and math classes. The principal was so impressed that he asked Babcock to take a full-time position when the math teacher retired. Babcock jumped at the chance. To get a Florida teaching license, however, he first had to leap through a series of hoops meant to prove that he was qualified to teach, never mind that his principal had already seen ample proof with real students. Luckily Babcock found a friendly expert in state licensure requirements at the district office. Following her advice, he took seven courses from four different colleges to complete a licensing program in time for the new school year.

In light of Babcock's experience and the principal's endorsement, such courses seemed unnecessary. Besides, Babcock had already devised his own lesson plans and methods. During his year as an aide, he had observed the school's best teachers and queried them about their teaching strategies. He learned the job by watching good teachers teach, not by spending seat time in courses on pedagogy.

How many eager, able, nontraditional teacher candidates like Bill Babcock do we lose because of our system of hoops and hurdles and red tape? How many gifted teachers do we lose because they throw up their hands in despair at the obstacles, costs, and coursework between them and the classroom?

At a time when public education suffers from a dual crisis of quantity and quality in its teaching ranks, bold action is needed. But of what sort? Educators contend that there is only one solution. Insisting that their goal is quality improvement, they urge tighter regulation of teacher training programs and even more hurdles to clear on the way to certification. Although well meaning, such proposals are not based on sound management or research.

Today's convergence of teacher shortages, teacher quality concerns, and toughened school-level accountability creates a grand opportunity for commonsense strategies. If, instead of erecting more barriers, we were to eliminate the hoops and hurdles that discourage good candidates from entering the classroom, we would find effective teachers in many places.

Charter schools, alternative schools, and private schools point the way. They're generally free to hire both licensed and unlicensed teachers, depending on state rules, to set their own terms of employment and to pay what the market will bear (within budgetary constraints). About 65 percent of teachers at private secular schools are not certified (Finn and Madigan 2001). Yet they are more likely to have graduated from selective colleges and universities, and therefore, to be broadly educated and to know their subject matter.

In the first year of Arizona's Phoenix Advantage Charter School, the physical education teacher was a world-class decathlete and the music teacher was a professional musician. Both had college degrees, neither held a teaching license. Both were very successful teaching their students.

Today's college graduates have many career options and opportunities. If the path into teaching is too burdensome or costly, they won't take it.

A recent study found two major reasons for college graduates choosing fields other than teaching: They wanted careers where their salary would keep pace with their performance, and they didn't want to return to school to take education courses that have questionable value (Farkas, Johnson, and Foleno 2000).

Managers suggest solutions to both problems. Rather than paying all teachers from the same scale without regard to their effectiveness, a district can devise innovative compensation schemes. A district could offer higher pay for teachers in hard-to-staff schools and in such shortage fields as math, science, and special education.

Solving the second problem draws managers into the quagmire of teacher training and certification. Conventional wisdom holds that to improve teacher preparation and quality, we should increase the time spent in training programs and the number of courses taken by future teachers. An alternative approach would be lowering the barriers to public school teaching by creating multiple pathways into the field.

Alternative certification, now flourishing in a few states and communities is one route. Many districts are experimenting with private programs like Teach for America, which places liberal arts graduates in public schools in poor rural communities as well as in the inner cities. Another program, Troops to Teachers, has placed more than 3000 military veterans in the classroom since 1994. The United States has also witnessed a surge in alternative certification programs, now available in at least forty states (Wolk 2001).

In Texas, school districts have begun to develop their own programs in teacher shortage areas. Virginia's Board of Education recently approved a program called Career Switches. Colorado allows districts and counties to offer fast-track programs. More states and districts are working with private companies, such as Sylvan Learning Systems and the New Teacher Project (a Teach for America spin-off) to create alternative routes to certification.

What most of these programs have in common are the requirements that a candidate possess a bachelor's degree, pass a competency examination and a background check, and complete a compressed training program that includes intensive, hands-on experience. After initial training, the new teacher usually receives support from a mentor teacher or supervisor. Although they're criticized by teacher's unions and colleges of education, these programs are opening doors for many individuals interested in becoming teachers.

As we open doors, we should demand more school-level accountability and make sure it touches the adults in a school, not just the students. All principals should be accountable for the educational performance of their students and be given the freedom to staff their schools as they think best. This includes discussions about whom to hire, retain, or remove. A principal may select a certified teacher, a former private school teacher, or a career changer with alternative certification. Making such decisions should be a key part of the manager or leader's job. The manager or leader is in the best position to assess how well an individual will match the school's mission and vision, and meet the student's needs.

Analysts generally agree that an effective school needs a cohesive staff with a shared vision and that tying the hands of the school's leader with respect to personnel makes it unreasonable to hold the leaders accountable for the school's performance (Ballou and Podgursky 2001; Cawell 1999). As we demand higher student performance, we obviously need more effective schools. That means schools with highly skilled teaching staffs.

The students at Ormond Beach Middle School were lucky. They had a principal, a district manager, and a teacher who were willing to plow through the regulatory roadblocks. But we can't count on exceptions to make the rule. While holding schools and teachers accountable for results, common sense still tells us to open some windows, to widen the pathways into the profession, to experiment with teacher compensation plans, and to empower principals to make personnel decisions. The conventional wisdom deserves to be tried, but so does common sense.

Alternative training programs for new and second career teachers offer a nontraditional way to address teacher shortages in high needs schools. Alternative models aim to get teachers into the classroom as soon as possible and do not discourage teachers from leaving the classroom to pursue other avenues for social change. Traditional programs take more time to develop skillful, confident teachers who will succeed and stay in the classroom. Both have a valid and increasingly necessary role.

But whether trained traditionally in a university setting or initially in a fast-track alternative, new teachers need meaningful preparation, ongoing support and collaboration, and a variety of incentives to keep them in the field. Those who recruit new teachers need to remember that they are not just responsible for the next generation of teachers, but also for the future of our schools.

The educational system is looking at preparing second-career teachers. Those teachers who switch into the profession from other fields bring maturity, experience, and commitment. Comprehensive, accelerated teacher preparation programs provide these teachers with knowledge, skills, and support.

The data are clear. Public schools in the United States are facing a teacher shortage that is projected to grow during the next ten years. Educators and community members have cause for concern about who will teach America's children. One solution may be to recruit and train individuals in other professional fields who are interested in becoming teachers.

As the teacher shortage worsens, substantial federal and state resources are being channeled into teacher recruitment and preparation efforts. Second career teachers emerge as viable candidates. In addition to breadth and depth of content knowledge, teachers entering the field at an older age have lower attrition rates than those entering at a younger age. Mid-career individuals bring many strengths to teaching, including maturity, life experience, and good work habits. Second career teachers are able to give real-world answers to the age-old student question, "Why do we have to learn this?" They are assertive and determined. Although many midcareer changes have extensive experience working in bureaucracies, they have limited patience with bureaucratic procedures and paperwork that they perceive as barriers to their work with the students. Midcareer individuals understand the realities of the workplace within the global economy and want to do their best to prepare students to be successful adults.

Another method of recruiting teachers is to help immigrants become teachers. Our immigrants are diverse within themselves. The largest ethnic communities within the United States have individuals from Ethiopia, Somalia, Vietnam, and Serbia, with students also from Russia, Iran, India, Indonesia, and Mexico. Many immigrants were middle-class intellectuals in their countries of origin, many hold university degrees, and some were teachers, principals, and university instructors. Very few of their professional credentials are recognized in the United States. Ketil Eiane, a graduate of the University of Oslo in Norway, is working as a teacher's aide because his master's degree in teaching is not recognized in the United States. Individuals like Ketil are ripe for recruitment. These immigrants bring expertise and rich life stories.

One man from Sudan taught business accounting in Liberia for five years before the outbreak of civil war in bordering countries sent refugees into Liberia. He was then trained by the United Nations task force to become a child trauma counselor in the refugee camps before he came to the United States. A woman from Serbia had taught high school English for eight years. One woman holds two bachelor's degrees from India where she taught third grade for two years. Another woman was attending the university in Iran, training to become a teacher when her family had to flee to Turkey. She taught English to adults in the refugee camps in Turkey for nearly five years before coming to the United States where she found work as a language facilitator in the public schools. These immigrants can provide cultural insights and real life experiences that can educate us all.

Cultural nuances can get lost in the daily business of schools and class-rooms. Having teachers who are aware of such subtleties from personal experience enriches the educational environment for all students and teachers.

WHO'S IN OUR CLASSROOMS?

Walking through the classroom door has cast me into a world where I am charged with the awesome responsibility of sculpting young minds and preparing students for positive participation in their communities.

Many teachers respond to the question of why they entered the teaching profession with, "I wanted a chance to make a positive change in the world." In my case, perhaps selfishly, I wanted to be in a profession that would make a positive change in me.

The following teacher essays were compiled by Carol Tell (2001), senior associate editor of *Educational Leadership*, and by personal interviews I conducted in 2002–2003.

The Gift, Elizabeth Hinde (sixth grade teacher, Porter Elementary School, Mesa, Arizona)

There they sat, all twenty-seven of them. It was the first day of school of my last year of teaching. I had taken a sabbatical the previous year to complete the coursework for my doctorate. To tell the truth, I did not want to go back to the classroom. I had grown tired of the committees, bus duties, and mandates from well-intentioned but out-of-touch legislators and administrators. Going back to teaching sixth graders, a job I had done for seventeen years, did not appeal to me anymore. But I went back and stood in front of the kids who had that look of expectancy that all students have on the first day of school, as if a gift were about to be opened for them.

So I started teaching. It felt as if I had put on an old sweatshirt: comfortable, warm, and feeling right. Throughout the year I told stories of ancient cultures until the students wanted to learn history. I read books to them that made them want to read more. I taught geography, the parts of a sentence, and the nature of the ocean until they wanted to travel, write, and swim. They reminded me that I did not become a teacher for the duties and committees and certainly not for the mandates from on high. I became a teacher for the kids.

Learning from Tyla

Tyla is an eighteen-year-old student with a two-month-old baby, living with her grandmother, mother, sister, two brothers, auntie, and a nephew in a two-bedroom house in the projects. She had outstanding traffic tickets that had turned into a warrant for her arrest. Although Tyla wanted to pursue her goals, she knew she had to turn herself in to the police and serve her punishment. Over Christmas vacation she handed her baby over to me, turned herself in to the police, and spent her vacation in jail, "sitting out" her tickets. When she got out she successfully finished high school, completed job training, and got a job.

I came into this profession to influence my students so that they might achieve their potential. As it turns out, they teach me every day. The Tylas of the world are the reason I am teaching and administrating our children.

Sneaking in the Lesson, Bruce Turnbaugh (high school social studies teacher, Heart of the Earth Center for American Indian Education, Minneapolis, Minnesota)

I began teaching more than thirty-five years ago. The students sat at their desks and didn't talk or move. They were to be seen and not heard, learn the lesson, and give it back on a test. I taught them from the outside in. Now I listen to them. I look for ways to sneak information into their heads. I teach while sitting in a boat on a lake taking students fishing. I let them know that they are important and accepted for who they are.

I have learned what love is. It is something you do and not something you get. A teacher must love the profession as well as the students.

The Right Stuff, Ona Kingbird (cultural teacher, Heart of the Earth Center for American Indian Education, Minneapolis, Minnesota)

I entered into teaching to help students learn some content about their culture and heritage. I found the students hungry to learn. Now I remain in teaching to teach students. My mission is to help students learn how to learn and to inspire them. I do this by challenging them to give their best efforts when they think that they do not have the "right stuff" for learning and success.

The Incredible Students

I stay in teaching and education for Steven, Ashley, Sonny, Cassandra, and Josh. Steven, who in seventh grade wrote, "The most valuable thing that we did this year was service learning/community service. Helping clean up the block was awesome. People looked at us differently." I stay for Ashley who confided that the best thing she read this year was *Death: Be Not Proud*, because it made her realize that other people have also lost loved ones and that she and her family were not alone in the world.

I have other reasons for staying in education: Jarvis, Jovan, D. Vince, Margaret, Sherrylynn, Alyssa—each with their own minds, needs, and stories. Each presents a new challenge and even though our interactions are not always pleasant, they are always meaningful. I'm where I need to be to help kids and that's what education is all about.

La Maestra, Maria Sanchez (Eastside Elementary School, Los Angeles, California)

Every year I am blessed with fresh-faced kindergarten children. I am awed by the knowledge that each child brings to the learning community. I am drawn into their learning. My students challenge me and I rise to the challenge.

Da Bomb, Kanesha Lee Baynard (Spanish teacher, Thornridge High School, Dolton, Illinois)

I am the super-energetic educator, "da bomb," the inspirer, the nurturer. I am the one who will stop my students and say, "Now I know that your Mama taught you better than that." I am the one trying to keep it together in the classroom while the school is falling apart in committee meetings. I am the personal stylist who says, "Now if you are going to wear that dress to the prom, you must have the correct undergarments." I am the one who reminds my students that out in the real world they will need skills that will set them apart from the other fun, cute, wily, and smart job candidates. I am the one who will stop a student in the hallway so that we can analyze just why profanity is not acceptable in our loud but respectful hallways. I am the one who reflects on the day during the commute home and sheds a tear every so often because my efforts seem so useless and the job becomes too much. But in the morning, I am the teacher who returns to class ready to change the world all over again.

A New Year, Karen Miller (second and third grade teacher, Wilsonville Primary School, West Linn, Oregon)

Each September, school takes me by surprise, and I wonder how to begin. I have discovered that although I may know where we are headed, with skills and concepts in mind, exactly how we will get there will be determined by the children who join me as a community of learners. The excitement and challenges begin. Trust and risk join hands.

I have come to trust children. With supportive structures in place, the children will respond with enthusiasm to the challenge of learning. They will handle the frustration inherent in real problem solving and emerge with pride and new understanding. Children who have opportunities to work together, to share success and the difficulties, and to become resources to one another, come to value one another's thinking and individuality.

First Year Blues, LaMar Elliot (high school English teacher, VOA Alternative High School, Minneapolis, Minnesota)

During my first year as a high school English teacher, I was about to admit defeat. One day, while reading a poem by Langston Hughes, my eyes—now trained to quickly scan the room for disruptions—finally opened to see a different angle in the classroom. Just as I was about to reprimand a talker, I looked into the eyes of a student staring quietly at me, patiently waiting to hear the next line of the poem. His eyes shone with sincere interest. My heart stopped. I was struck by the realization that I had been ignoring the quiet students who diligently did their work and paid attention.

From that point, I ignored minor disruptions and put my energy toward the students who actually followed my directions and displayed an interest in literature. The tone of the class changed. The students with a desire to learn started to bloom. One student said that she loved poetry, another said I was great. These comments sent my heart soaring. I was managing my classroom. I was a teacher.

Key to the Future, Jaime Castellano (administrator, Gifted Education Program, Palm Beach County, Florida)

Raised in a poor Mexican barrio of Chicago's Southeast Side, I learned quickly that education was the key to the future. I have worked to identify gifted and talented students who come from culturally diverse backgrounds and attend school in our most poverty-stricken communities. So far we have identified almost four hundred students in only ten schools dispelling the myth that gifted and talented students could not be found in these communities. I am confident that our work will make a difference to the education of this generation and future generations.

Attitude, Marcus Allen (fourth, fifth, and sixth grade teacher, VOA Elementary School, Minneapolis, Minnesota)

Pride fills my heart as my students talk about the inequalities of the Jim Crow Laws and what American Indians had to endure on the reservations and the aftereffects that have a negative impact on our society. My aim for more than ten years has been to provoke thought, effect change, and instill pride in *all* children to enable them to carry on the message that indeed all people are created equal.

Someone said, "Attitude determines attitude." It is my hope and belief that what I do really matters and that, somehow, the message gets across to my students and elevates them through language and deed. Prejudice and racism continue to pervade America's society, and I must do what I can to eradicate these ills.

These short paragraphs clearly show teachers involved in their professions and schools. Managers must involve teachers in the life of the school. I'm not talking about site-based management but about teachers studying one another's lessons the way the Japanese do, visiting classes, presenting case studies about hard-to-teach kids, advising one another. I'm talking about the involvement of teachers in the life of their schools, their communities, their kids, and the decisions about curriculum. Too many teachers show up in the morning and go home in the afternoon. They have nothing to do with the life of their school.

Unless we change working conditions allowing teachers to participate more in planning the curriculum, choosing tests, and running the schools, thoughtful professionals are going to abandon their careers. When this happens we have a serious problem called out-of-field teaching. The statistics about out-of-field teaching are shocking. Only 41 percent of those who teach math have a math teaching license or even a degree in mathematics (Berliner 2001). However, is that so bad? Midcareer teachers and those who change their careers to become teachers have a wealth of knowledge to offer students. There is no reason that these individuals should not become successful teachers. Experience is worth considering when judging the success of teachers.

Out-of-field teaching is a tremendous problem for minority school districts and for rural school districts. We can solve this problem by recruiting and paying the candidates we need. Industry complains about out-of-field teachers but industry is stealing our mathematicians.

Teachers are reacting by growing toward the profession.The following are suggestions for all teachers:

- Analyze your memories of successful teachers and successful learning experiences to discover how you can teach effectively.
- Ensure wholeness in your life by blending your plans for professional and personal growth.
- Analyze a range of teaching styles to find the most effective for you.
- Realize students learn differently by reflecting on the ways you and your friends learned best.
- Assess your preferences for classroom management approaches.
- Use classroom visits and observations to assess the teaching styles of others.
- Share information, use reflective practices, and add action research.
- Build on success.
- Keep your focus on the future and on the excitement of life-long learning.
- Investigate new technologies and how you can best use them.

Teachers need to change the public's perception of teachers. Teachers need to provide more leadership, be more politically active, and show concern about the community. Teachers can share their intellectual skills with the public by writing letters to the editor of their local papers and by speaking at public meetings. No one else can change the perception of teachers except teachers themselves. There are over three million teachers. Let's get out there and fight for recognition.

For students to consistently learn well, students need to be respected, believe that what they are learning is relevant to their needs, and believe that they can master what they are being asked to learn.

Remember, "A mind stretched by a new idea will never return to its original position" (Don Coyhis, founder, White Bison, Inc.). This is what teaching is all about.

7

The Media Monster

Nothing in life is to be feared. It is only to be understood.

—Marie Curie

Educators must make communication a priority if they are to gain public support. There are many practical ways one can forge better links between school leaders and the community. First, always listen. Then focus on internal audiences. Use effective messengers and messages. Make communications a strategic priority. In other words, communicate with the so-called media monster—the news media, television reporters, and journalists who are looking for sensational stories about schools that will bring in readers and viewers.

Listen first. Today's parents and, indeed, all voters, need to see and hear about signs of success if they are to support public schools. But their ideas of success often differ from the agendas of educational reformers.

In many districts, the public looks first at what we call the "three Bs"—books, bathrooms, and bureaucracy. The public wants their school-age children to have the books they are supposed to have, they want the bathrooms in schools to be clean and safe, and they want the administrative bureaucracy to be trimmed. The public expects districts to address these core issues before they are ready for deeper conversations about higher standards, challenging curriculum, and restructured schools. The media often asks: What would the readers and listeners need to see that would indicate that schools are improving? Then they listen for answers like higher test scores, higher graduation rates, higher levels of engagement for parents and children, improved safety, and smaller class sizes.

We must focus on internal audiences. A primary communications problem in most school districts is with internal audiences, those people who work for the school districts. This audience is often not adequately informed to do their jobs or to be good communicators themselves. They get their information from local newspapers or the rumor mill, rarely from their employer. The districts can build greater levels of public support if instead of informing only the superintendent and board members, it has an informed cadre of communicators who talk positively about schools with their neighbors at supermarkets, on soccer fields, and in barber shops.

Schools should use effective messages and messengers. Watching education leaders and managers try to explain their programs to nonexpert audiences is painful. Their language is often complicated, their sentences complex and hard to follow. They get to the point slowly and speak on an abstract level. Educational leaders need to develop the communication discipline to produce messages that work, to explain about their schools and programs in plain, understandable language. They need to understand that less is really more. A paragraph can be more effective than a whole page.

Words matter. So do images. Much of communications is emotional rather than intellectual. Managers are trained to see the picture. Engage people through stories, symbols, and pictures. One good story about a child's success and his or her teacher's high expectations is more likely to connect with audiences than a discourse on the value of world-class standards to the competitive position of the United States in the global economy of the twenty-first century. Take a blossoming student and an effective teacher to a meeting with the local newspapers or the business luncheon, and you will see the impact.

Make communications a strategic priority. Most schools have a strategic plan focused on improving student achievement. This puts communication in the direct service of student achievement. Ask the key question: What do you need from which segment of your public to succeed?

Talk to the so-called media monster. Talk radio can ruin your day before it starts. Anyone responsible for communicating news about a school or school district will recognize the following scenario:

6:00 a.m.: You open one eye to the sound of an announcer's voice proclaiming, "Police have charged two Anytown High School students with assaulting another youth with a weapon during a gang fight yesterday." By the time you open your other eye, the voice has moved on to news of a traffic accident without a further explanation of the incident involving your students.

6:10 a.m.: You call the newsroom to check the source of the story. After punching directed numbers you reach voicemail, so you keep trying. You finally reach a newscaster who says the details are correct. The boys were involved in a relatively minor fight (no injuries) in the parking lot of a local shopping mall with a group (not a gang) of other teenagers. The "weapon" was a baseball bat that one boy was putting in his car when the fight broke out. The incident had no connection with the school, which was not even mentioned in the police report. The newscaster now agrees that the first early morning version might have been misleading.

6:20 a.m.: The superintendent calls, "Did I miss something yesterday? Did we have a gang-related incident?" "No." And "No. I'm working on it."

6:30 a.m.: A second newscast reports the fight did not happen at the school. However, this subtle change did not satisfy principals, teachers, and parents who simply equate the school name with violence.

7:25 a.m.: The principal from another Anytown High School calls. She didn't hear either news version but has heard several other versions from her teachers and from others who have called. You give her the facts and hope that it is not a slow news day. You don't need television cameras showing up outside the school. You also hope that the incident is too insignificant to have been picked up by a news wire service because correcting wire stories is like retrieving the proverbial feather in the wind.

8:00 a.m.: You start your day at the office by faxing the police report to the superintendent and the chairman of the school board (who heard the first version from a coworker) so that an accurate report (first-hand information) will be presented.

Before the day is over, you have talked to the police and press about a student caught distributing drugs, an employee who showed up for work drunk (an adult who saw the employee arrive at the school chose to make an anonymous call to a reporter instead of talking to you, the administrator), a minor bus accident, and a bomb threat (an anonymous student called the press) that caused the vacating of the school.

Educators who are aggravated by this type of routine reporting are likely to be too idealistic, too defensive, too naïve, or too paranoid about the press.

None of these attitudes fosters the effective, open communication that is essential for those educators who hope to increase the public support and understanding.

The public interest is best served when articulate, credible school leaders and spokespersons work closely with responsible, knowledgeable journalists. Most educators and journalists have enough common sense and goodwill to work together productively. For school leaders, that means working closely with the media to improve their access to information, their knowledge and understanding of educational issues, and the accuracy of their stories.

Today's administrators recognize that they work in the hot glare of a public spotlight. This role demands a new sensitivity to the relative roles of a free public education and a free press in a democracy. No other form of communication available to educators can reach the broad audience called the public as effectively as the media. Therefore, use the media to your advantage.

8

The Awesome School

We must do the things we think we cannot do. The future belongs to those who believe in the beauty of their dreams.

—Eleanor Roosevelt

In the early twentieth century, philosopher and scientist Otto Neurath envisioned managers as sailors who on the open sea must reconstruct their sinking ship but are never able to start from the bottom. They must make use of some drifting timber of the old structure, but they cannot put the ship to dock to start from scratch. During their work they stay on the old structure and deal with gales and thundering waves (Sterman 1995, 1). This is a wonderful metaphor for the challenge we face in a world of ever-accelerating change. We must learn about complex systems that have grown increasingly dangerous, all the while living in the midst of these systems.

In the words of John Dewey in *A Common Faith* (1934):

We who now live are part of a humanity that extends into the remote past, a humanity that has interacted with nature. The things in civilization we most prize are not of ourselves. They exist by grace of the doings and sufferings of the continuous human community in which we are a link. Ours is the responsibility of conserving, transmitting and rectifying and expanding of the heritage of values we have received that those who come after us may receive it more solid and secure, more widely accessible and more generously shared than we have received it.

A persistent impulse that should not be disregarded ran deep among the great progressives. That impulse was the firm conviction that democracy is possible, that the democratic way of life can be lived, and that our schools should and can bring democracy to life in the curriculum, in school governance, in community relations, and in the hearts and minds of young people. That idea of democracy was not an empty shell, nor was it based on the vulgar notion of a free marketplace of competing alternatives from which people choose whatever suits their self-interest and their bank accounts. Instead, democracy was to involve intelligent, collaborative participation in society. Creative individuality was to be balanced with concern for the welfare of others and a desire for a common good. Human dignity, equity, justice, and caring were to serve as both ends and means in our political, economic, and social relations. Practices like these and the urge for democracy that drove them reflect a noble impulse that is worth reclaiming today.

To dismiss the history of that impulse, I would have to dismiss my own experience during my first years of teaching when I came into contact with some of those "old" progressives. I remember conversations about the rights of young people, democratic classrooms, how students could help plan the curriculum, how we could give social issues a larger place in the curriculum, the unfairness of standardized tests, and the despicable injustices that crushed the souls of children. We were not afraid. We were part of a long line of progressive work.

Today the talk about teaching and learning is mostly about something else entirely. We may want to wish otherwise, but it cannot be denied. The standards movement is in full swing, as are the national testing schemes. The long list of facts and skills they entail are mistakenly called a curriculum, and the definition of curriculum planning itself is reduced to the managerial function of aligning standards, tests, lesson plans, and all the rest of the authoritarian mechanisms needed to control young people and their teachers. We are led to worship test scores, the false idols of education. And although the metaphorical bar has been raised for our children, politicians, bureaucrats, and educators have explicitly refused to ensure that every school, and therefore, every child, will have equitable resources to accomplish the standards.

Schools are examples of educational boutiques, where parents are "consumers" of the teaching "product." We make new programs for the affluent that will reaffirm their cultural dominance and separate their children from those who are nonprivileged. We make new programs for parents who wish to hide from their children's view those who do not subscribe to their own beliefs. We make new programs to satisfy the labor needs of greedy corporations. In short, we act as if the schools are maintained merely to serve self-interests. We have become a profession of fads and glitzy programs, with no pedagogical or moral compass to guide us. I can only imagine the hurt and anger so many teachers must feel as they are blamed for problems in our schools, when, in fact, the real source lies in the movement to turn our schools and other public institutions over to private greed and political self-interest. Our teachers should not be at the center of our scrutiny. Instead, we must turn our attention to the conditions under which they are able to teach, the increasing stranglehold of authoritarian control, the insidious game of academic competition among students of different countries, the refusal to level the playing field of school resources, and the general failure of nerve in our society's social conscience. It is true that those conditions arise from movements outside our schools and that we must resist them. But it is just as true that they have invaded the curriculum within our schools.

It is time to reclaim a purpose for education that is worth living, one that demands or takes action. We should begin now to ask something more than the narrow economic and political purposes being forced upon us.

We should ask that the curriculum bring diverse groups of young people together in communities of learning where they can live and work together, where their diversity is a prized aspect of the group rather than a criterion for the sort-and-select machine. We should ask that the curriculum focus on topics that are of real significance to both students and the larger society. We should ask that the curriculum treat students with dignity, as real people who live in the real world and care about its condition and fate. We should ask that the curriculum value the knowledge and experience young people bring with them to school as well as what they think would be worth pursuing. Students should have a say about their own learning experiences and their say should really count for something.

We should ask that the curriculum engage important knowledge from many sources and be organized so that it is meaningful and accessible to young people. The rhythms and patterns of their inquiring minds ought to be more important in determining the scope and sequence of knowledge than the recommendations of academics who rarely see young people in schools or bureaucrats to whom they are only anonymous statistics in official reports. We want a curriculum that involves knowledge that is as rich in its diversity as our society.

We should ask that the curriculum bring our young people into contact with the most important and current ideas through the best resources we can find. We have an obligation to help our children become well informed. The curriculum must offer our young people a chance to critique existing knowledge and construct new meanings, accepting no fact as authoritative simply because it appears in a book or on the Internet. We should ask that the curriculum offer something better than short-answer standardized tests, for in their cold impersonalness these tests insult our humanity, trivialize our desires, and balkanize our young people. The goals and expectations must be reasonable and achievable for all young people.

We should ask that the curriculum be kind to young people, uplifting their hopes and their possibilities, instead of discouraging their spirits and aspirations. Its purpose should be to inspire them, not punish them. The work they do should involve more making and doing, more building and creating, and less of the deadening drudgery that too many of our curriculum arrangements still demand.

We should ask that the curriculum challenge our young people to imagine a better world and to try out ways of making it so. The curriculum should be better for our young people than it was for us. It should not simply be what we had in school but what we wished we could have had or, without prejudice, should have had.

This type of curriculum may invite ridicule. It is too idealistic, some would say. It is too dangerous, some would say, to give our children ideas like that. It is too ambiguous, some would say, for young people who should be told right or wrong answers. Others will ask, "Will it give businesses a competitive edge in the global economy?" "Will our students score as well as those in other countries on international comparison tests?" "Will they get into elite universities?" Our challenge is to do what is best for children and to recapture the meaningful purpose of teaching and learning.

Can we go back and quote Dewey and Giroux who said Americans have defined schooling as a public good and a fundamental right (Dewey 1916; Giroux 1998)? Is this part of the awesome school philosophy?

Awesome schools bring together people of diverse talents and perspectives so they can achieve common visions and take joint actions. Collaboration, team building, leadership, and management are critical pieces of these schools.

In awesome schools:

- Parents are integral members of the educational team.
- Curriculum promotes cultural competence and appreciates ethnic diversity.
- Instructional methods promote cooperation, interaction, and success for students.
- Assessment includes alternative methods that will allow for cultural differences and encourage community review to insure an equitable approval of students' work.
- The culture supports student growth and promotes oneness.
- There is assurance of quality education for children of poverty.
- Parents see clear-cut goals leading to improved academic performance.
- The learning environment is safe.
- Learning is in collaboration, not isolation.
- Teachers begin where children are, not at the front of a curriculum guide.
- Teachers are ready to engage students in instruction through different learning modalities by appealing to different interests and by using varied rates of instruction along with varied degrees of complexity.
- Teachers provide specific ways for each individual to learn as deeply as possible and as quickly as possible without assuming one student's roadmap for learning is identical to anyone else's.
- Students are held to high standards and come to believe that learning involves effort, risk, and personal triumph.
- Teachers use time flexibly, call upon a range of instructional strategies, and become partners with their students to shape the learning environment. They do not force-fit learners into a standard mold.
- Teachers are students of their students.
- Teachers unconditionally accept students as they are and expect them to become all that they can be.

Awesome schools look at differences in learning styles and make an adjustment in how all students are taught. Those schools develop innovative programs that meet the needs of the population they serve. By building on what students come with and know and by determining their learning styles schools can expand the knowledge and skills of the student they serve.

We think, learn, and create in different ways. The development of our potential is affected by the match between what we learn and how we learn. The awesome school is responsible for increased student achievement, and stipulates academic goals and student achievement methods.

The awesome school:

- Is aware of the continuing focus of racism, sexism, classism, and bias
- Is aware that equity in funding is a serious issue and discrepancies must be addressed
- Will do more partnering with public institutions, businesses, and foundations
- Fosters innovation through experimentation
- Uses a variety of educational approaches (interdisciplinary instruction, expanded use of technology, increased parental involvement, performance assessments, and portfolios)
- Exercises greater personal and professional judgment in creating exemplary educational programs
- Selects curriculum and an instructional delivery system that places students at the center
- Provides a setting permeated by a love of learning
- Has clear plans for how classrooms will be altered to enhance the teaching/learning process
- Empowers teachers to play key roles in determining the best educational program available for all students
- Stresses professional development (explores how adults learn)
- Gives parents the opportunity to be integral members of the educational team

The awesome schools are neither educational panaceas nor fads. They allow educators to combine genuine educational diversity and cutting-edge innovation with rigorous standards and accountability. And accountability is critical for all schools.

We must help all students achieve. We know that we are living in uncommon times for education when everyone from President Bush to the

Children's Defense Fund is championing the same slogan—in this case, *Leave No Child Behind.*

Although divergent in philosophy and political bent, liberal and conservative organizations from the Heritage Foundation to the Public Education Network to the Business Round Table agree on some practices that could narrow the achievement gap between the rich and the poor.

Improving the quality of instruction is the only way to improve overall student achievement. Teacher quality is the single most accurate indicator of a student's performance in school.

Teacher qualifications matter. Parents are concerned with how and where teachers get assigned. They want to see how well teachers know their subject matter and whether they can provide role models for their children.

To increase the achievement levels of minority and low-income students we need to focus on what really matters: high standards, a challenging curriculum, and qualified teachers.

Historically, we have not agreed on what American students should learn at each grade level or on what kind of work is good enough. These decisions have been left to individual schools and teachers. The result is a system that, by and large, doesn't ask much of its students. Ask the nearest teenager and in survey after survey young people tell us that they are not being challenged in school.

We are stunned by how little is expected of students in high poverty schools and how few assignments they get in a given school week. We are also stunned by the low level of the few assignments that they do get.

Clear and public standards for what students should learn at benchmark grade levels are a critical part of solving the problem. They are a guide—for teachers, administrators, parents, and students themselves—to what knowledge and skills students must master.

Standards won't make much of a difference if they are not accompanied by a rigorous curriculum that is aligned with those standards. How and why standards can improve student achievement is the focus of this next section.

STANDARDS AND ACHIEVEMENT

Many educators suggest that we cut the number of standards and breadth of content within standards dramatically. The sheer number of standards is the biggest impediment to implementing standards. The process of identifying standards has started a conversation about what students should know in different subject areas. Standards do not lessen the responsibility of educators to evaluate the performance of students and to report the results. The standards must be broad enough to allow for efficient communication of student learning, yet specific enough to be useful. Meanwhile, principals across the country are focusing on individualizing instruction. Principals say that teachers need to focus more on individual student needs and that schools need to provide more reading and math instruction to low-achieving students. Some suggestions are to look at the data, identify a reading program, and expand the schedule. Designate an uninterrupted reading or math block in the morning. Some principals group the entire school by ability during that time. Instead of one third grade teacher teaching reading to all her students, for example, students went to different teachers for their reading instruction on the basis of their test scores and assigned levels. The most common school academic program, however, is the extended day. Activities generally include after school tutoring, homework clubs, and remedial programs. Most students work in small groups with a teacher on either reading or math until they come up to grade level.

Standards can lead to an integrated curriculum. And an integrated curriculum enables students to see the big picture, to understand the topic's relevance and real-life context, and to engage in higher-order thinking skills. Teachers are enthusiastic. Strategies are chosen that are hands-on, offer variety, apply to real-life context, and promote critical thinking.

Standards exist for diverse learners as well. What kind of diversity exists in American classrooms?

- Students are no longer either Catholic, Jewish, or Protestant. In fact the fastest growing religion in the United States is Islam (Hodgkenson 1998).
- Most of the 5.3 million American students with disabilities spend some part of their day in mainstreamed classes (Kaye 1997).
- At least one-third of the school-aged population in the United States is nonwhite (Marlow and Page 1999).
- Forty-three million people in the United States move every year (Hodgkenson 1998).

In addition, trends such as multicultural education, antitracking pedagogy, inclusive education, dual-bilingual programs, magnet schools, and multi-age classrooms are contributing to the rich diversity of American schools. The standards movement will have little meaning if it cannot respond to the needs of all these students.

To make standards inclusive educators must support and cultivate five conditions:

1. Standards are developmental and flexible. Standards cannot be a one-size-fits-all approach to education. A student cannot and should not be expected to know and do exactly the same things as his or her peers.
2. Standards require a wide range of assessment tools (portfolios, interviews, observations, anecdotal records, self-evaluation questionnaires, journals, and learning logs).
3. Standards allow equitable access to meaningful content. We have not done a good job of giving all students, particularly those students with unique learning characteristics, access to an appealing, thought-provoking, and stimulating curriculum.
4. It takes a community to implement standards. Collaboration between general and special education can provide students with more opportunities to practice related skills. All students benefit from the different teaching approaches, instructional styles, and perspectives.
5. Standards are a catalyst for other reforms.

Standards are not the only route to education excellence but they can help us address the most pressing issues that stand in the way of students having a quality educational experience.

For standards to work, schools need caring, learning communities, skilled and responsive teachers, adequate financial, human, and material resources, effective partnerships with families, and concerned and visionary managers and leaders.

In order to educate effectively, you must look beyond what is affecting education. Ask yourself, what works? Ask school officials anywhere what they are doing to improve student achievement, and you will hear a litany of initiatives. But ask for evidence that the initiatives work and the answers become more tentative: "It's too soon to tell. . . ." "We're collecting data on that. . . ." "Teachers have been enthusiastic. . . ." Doesn't anyone know what works? Look around you. There are methods of improving student achievement that do work:

- Start early. Home backgrounds are responsible for roughly half of their school achievement.
- Focus on reading and mathematics. Kids who are not reading at grade level by the end of first grade face eight to one odds against ever catching up. Kindergarten and first grade should be about getting basic reading and math. As students get older, do not herd students into "math for dummies"; offer two math courses each semester so they can catch up.
- Bring in trained tutors for one-on-one help. Tap retired teachers for resources.
- Invest in teachers.
- Utilize technology.
- Shrink the sizes of classes and schools.
- Increase the amount of time spent learning.
- Assess student progress and set goals.
- Support teacher professional development. Investing in performance works.
- Invest based on well-documented evidence.
- Keep your eyes on a comprehensive, long-term plan that focuses on improved learning.
- Use the "best of the old" with the most promising of the new.

Investing in leaders for learning works. Your school governance team can support student achievement:

- Make trust the bottom line.
- Communicate, communicate, communicate.
- Get the right team players.
- Build a foundation for teamwork.
- Make sure the players know their roles.
- Build support on all levels.

Investing in parent support works. The key is to keep parent involvement from turning into parent interference. We all know that children are more likely to succeed in school when their parents are involved in their education. Administrators and teachers trust parents to have the knowledge and wisdom to help solve a child's problem, and parents trust teachers and other staff to care about their child and to make sound professional judgments. Parents trust smaller schools that contract out for school services like special education, finances, and state reporting.

All schools can learn from business. In fact, some business practices are right for schools. Should public schools operate like businesses? What could schools learn from business?

When it comes to the operational side of public education, in such areas as maintenance, purchasing, transportation, food service, and the like, adopting business practices might improve both the effectiveness and the efficiency of our public schools. A dozen schools in Colorado explored this notion. Auditors used by businesses and corporations came in to look at the schools as though they were companies and explored how these schools could save time and money.

The auditors' recommendations fell into four categories: accountability, business orientation, communication coordination and cooperation, and cost effectiveness. The auditors also addressed such issues as workflow, staff responsibilities, and salaries.

The most useful recommendations to come out of this scenario were:

- Communication and coordination among departments. Workflow varies during the year and cross-training makes it easy to shift employees to the departments that need them the most, thus reducing the need to hire part-time staff. With cross-training the employees learn about the responsibility and function of personnel in other areas, which leads to improved communication. This is workable among school departments.
- Clear lines of responsibility. Problems may arise where no clear lines of responsibility exist. Who is responsible for what?
- Market-driven salaries. Be competitive.
- Work assignments. Address assignment of responsibility in relation to pay levels and competency.
- Privatization and outsourcing. Allow schools to purchase services from private sources if they believe that the cost and quality of these services are better than those from school personnel.

Schools can learn from business. Schools have important information on program costs and operational needs, thus being able to make decisions on how to use resources. Schools need to learn how to minimize duplication and increase accountability. As we learn from business, however, I caution schools to consider all options carefully. Schools are more deeply intertwined in the culture of the community than most businesses. Schools are also expected to operate humanely and provide stable employment. Attitude, behavior, and communication—all found in successful business models—are the ABCs from which a school can create a customer-friendly environment that welcomes and serves all its constituents.

Business expressions like *marketing* and *customer service* are just beginning to infiltrate educational jargon, yet many educators are not comfortable with the invasion. Educators usually do not think of our services in terms of customers. However, with the rise of choice—charter schools, alternative schools, magnet schools, and vouchers—a decidedly commercial concept has begun to change the rules: competition. Today's schools cannot afford to ignore its implications for the way they relate to their customers.

If we accept, either graciously or grudgingly, that competition means that schools must adopt a market-driven approach, how do we determine who our customers are? Are they our students (certainly the focus of our services)? Their parents (usually our most compelling patrons)? The tax paying public (they do pay the bills)? And what about teachers, administrators, and staff? Don't they count?

Yes to all of the above. Anyone who interacts with a school could and should be considered its customers. And all should be treated in ways that embody a customer-friendly approach toward realizing the goals and values of our schools. However, in today's competitive environment, parents and other taxpayers ultimately determine how and whether schools stay in business. They are the purchasers of educational services for our youth. By definition, then, they are our primary customers.

How can schools best serve their customers? The ultimate measure of service is the quality of the product. However, certain supporting practices can either advance or hinder the core educational mission—attitude, behavior, and communication. The good news is that these practices do not require much time or money.

Attitude: People don't care how much you know until they know how much you care. Consider this scenario at Anywhere Elementary School:

The voice on the other end of the line is flat and perfunctory. I can hear another phone in the background. "Can you hold, please?" Before I can respond, I am put on hold. As I wait I realize that I am put off by the person who answered the call. I feel like an intruder, an inconvenience. But why? In today's busy office environment, it is not unusual to be put on hold.

Then I realize that it is not so much *what* she did, but *how* she did it. The tone and tempo of her voice, the lack of inflection and or pause for a response, suggested that she was not thrilled to get my call. Whether she meant it or not, she gave the impression that she didn't care. She could have left a more positive impression simply by putting a smile in her voice, varying her inflection, and waiting for my response. These are small, easy to learn changes, but what a difference they make.

Behavior: It is not what you do but how you do it. Next scenario: The woman stood silently at the school office counter. Both secretaries were busy, one on the phone, the other with a sick child. A teacher entering the office noticed the woman and brightly asked whether he could help her. It was apparent the woman spoke little English. Undaunted, the teacher offered a few words in broken Spanish. Nodding and gesturing animatedly they walked down the hallway.

First impressions are vital and often indelible. The essence of effective customer service behavior is courtesy, which the dictionary defines as polite, helpful, and considerate behavior.

Communication: You never get a second chance to make a first impression. Can your school's main entrance sign be read from a distance? Is your school's mission statement attractively displayed through exhibits of student work? What sounds do you hear when you walk the halls? Your school's environment says a lot about your school. It is a silent messenger about the attitudes and behaviors contained within its walls. Your school's grounds and buildings, even its sounds and odor, communicate how much its occupants care and what they care about. The environment is an essential component of customer service.

Another important aspect of customer-oriented communication is listening. To serve your customer well, you must know what the customer wants and needs. Ask, and be open to input. Give customers multiple opportunities to give feedback on your services. Listen carefully and don't be defensive. Take all ideas into consideration, regardless of their merit. Most people will respect the results even if they don't agree, as long as they feel they have been heard. The essence of good customer service is showing that you care.

Remember, in today's competitive environment, your school's success and survival may depend on how well you serve your customers. It is easier to strive for success when teachers and administrators work with individuals, coaching and supporting them through difficult stages. It is easier to succeed when school employees show they genuinely care.

As educators, it is important to confront the issues by resurrecting the noble tradition extending from Horace Mann to Martin Luther King, Jr., in which education is affirmed as a political process that encourages people to identify themselves as more than consumers, and education as more than a spectacle of market culture.

Given the current assault on educators at all levels of schooling, educators must also struggle against the ongoing trend to reduce teachers to the role of technicians who simply implement prepackaged curricula and standardized tests as part of the efficiency-based relations of market-driven consumer pedagogy.

Teachers need to have the power and autonomy to function as intellectuals working under conditions that give them the time to produce curricula, engage in dialogues with students, use the resources of the community, and participate in the organizational decisions that affect their work.

Teachers I have interviewed about what makes an awesome school embraced the following four beliefs:

1. Respect the readiness level of each student.
2. Expect all students to grow and support their continued growth.
3. Offer all students the opportunity to explore essential understandings and skills at degrees of difficulty that escalate consistently as they develop their understanding and skill.
4. Offer tasks that look and are equally interesting, equally important, and equally engaging.

Teachers should be defended as public intellectuals who provide an indispensable service to the nation.

To create awesome schools we all need to become change agents. The following are tips for those wishing to embrace the concept of becoming a change agent:

- Be open to data at the start. Even if you think you know what you're doing, chances are you do not know what you could be doing. Open up your mind to as much innovative thinking as you can absorb. You may find different and better ideas than your school currently uses.
- Network like crazy. There is a network of people who are thinking about change. I've found that you can get in touch with them easily. I've had people say, "I can't believe you talked to so-and-so. How did you do it?" The answer is, "I called him!"
- Document your own learning. Others in the school need to see documentation for their own comfort. The smartest thing I did was to create a manual of ideas from leading managers and leaders and innovative thinkers. I documented two categories of thinking, the elements of a learning organization, and the pitfalls to avoid.
- Take others in management along. It helps to show that other schools are actually doing some of the same learning practices.
- No fear! You must be fearless and not worry about playing the game to keep your position.
- Never stop learning. Be a learning person yourself. Change agents are in love with learning and are consistently learning new things themselves. They find new ways to communicate those things to the school.
- Laugh when it hurts. This can be very discouraging work. You need a good sense of humor. It also helps if you have a mantra you can say to yourself when things are not going well. I say to myself, "We live for the next headache."
- Know the school before you try to change it. I don't think you can be successful if you are just a theorist. Have an understanding of the teachers and staff and what they can do.
- Finish what you start. I've made lists of change projects that were started in the past and never finished. I called it "the black hole." I determined early on that I did not want to be part of a second-rate movie.

As we look at schools in the twenty-first century, we find that many are spending more on administration and less on instruction. Student performance is not improving and sometimes appears worse. We only need a few schools to be incubators of reform as we search for more student achievement, accountability, and innovation. The solutions will not be found in Washington, D.C.; they will be found in cities and towns across the nation under those with leadership and managerial skills.

Sometimes leadership is presented in such favorable language and management is presented as such a prosaic activity that the two might be seen as in conflict with one another or as polarized. On the contrary, schools need supervisors who fulfill both leadership and management roles. Sometimes leadership and management talent reside in the same person; at other times, those talents are found in different people. Leadership alone will not get the job done; there must be a manager—someone to administer schedules, complete reports, and manage budgets and resources.

The differences between the two sets of talents can be starkly differentiated as though polarized at two extremes of management activity, represented in table 8.1.

In practice we can see how the two sets of talents can be brought together into a more realistic and productive harmony. Table 8.2 shows the collaboration of leadership and managerial talent.

Skill sets go hand in hand with the talents highlighted in table 8.2 and are needed by individuals who are both managers and leaders. The following are skill sets I feel are critical for the twenty-first century manager and leader if we are going to create awesome schools:

- Ability to understand the culture of the school
- Ability to let go of myths

Table 8.1. Talents of Leaders and Managers

Leader	Manager
Concerned with growth	Concerned with maintenance
Director	Stage manager
Writes the script	Follows the script
Reflects moral authority	Reflects legal and bureaucratic authority
Challenges people	Keeps people happy
Has vision	Keeps tests, schedules, and budgets
Exercises power of shared purpose	Exercises power of sanctions and rewards
Defines what is real as what is possible	Defines what is real as what is
Motivates	Controls
Inspires	Fixes
Illuminates	Coordinates

Table 8.2.   Collaboration of Leadership and Managerial Talents

Leader	Leader/Manager	Manager
Concerned with growth	Concerned with instructional growth	Concerned with maintenance
Director	Engages in reflective practice management	Stage manager
Writes the script	Communicates the meaning of the script	Follows the script
Challenges people	Channels challenges into fulfilling and productive programs	Keeps people happy
Has vision	Institutionalizes vision	Keeps lists, schedules, and budgets
Exercises power of shared purpose	Enables power of professional and moral community	Exercises power of sanctions and rewards
Defines what is real and what is possible	Defines reality as what is possible for now, for our circumstances tomorrow may be different	Defines what is real as what is
Motivates	Facilitates reflective practice	Organizes
Inspires	Encourages	Fixes
Illuminates	Cheerleads, celebrates	Coordinates

- Ability to notice new patterns, positive and negative, in teachers and students (multitasking, miniaturization, short-term memory overload, low level depression, changes of speed)
- Ability to develop a clear and open perspective (relax, laugh, know your history)
- Ability to examine what leaders reward, evaluate, control, and measure
- Ability to generate energy with coaching and building self-esteem
- Ability to learn forever
- Ability to own your career
- Ability to create safe environments for others
- Ability to see what is coming and what is leaving so you can make responsible choices

Despite compelling new educational knowledge, traditional public schools have changed little over the past one hundred years. The assumption remains that a child of a given age is enough like all other children of the same age that he or she should traverse the same curriculum in the same fashion with all other students of that age. Further, schools act as though all children should finish classroom tasks as near to the same moment as possible. Howard Gardner has contributed greatly to the awareness that students vary in intelligence preferences or strengths. While Gardner is clear that intelligences are interrelated, he is also convinced that there are important differences among them (Gardner 1983).

Schools of the twenty-first century must foster classrooms where excellent teaching is targeted to the variable learning needs of diverse students. Many teachers today still contend with the essential challenge of the single-room school. How do we reach out effectively to students who span the spectrum of learning readiness, personal interests, and culturally shaped ways of seeing, speaking in, and experiencing that world? The biggest mistake of past centuries in teaching has been to treat all children as if they were variants of the same individual and thus feel justified in teaching them the same subjects in the same ways. Schools need to feel right to students who learn in different ways at different rates and who bring to school different talents and interests.

Teaching about and from the cultures of all students is more than a political statement, it is sound educational theory. Students construct knowledge by incorporating new understanding with the knowledge they bring into the classroom.

Public schools were created on the premise that education would be the great social equalizer. Yet due to inertia or tradition, too few schools are preparing children to compete in the twenty-first century. Managers stress change and yet change is the most talked about and the least acted upon concept in the school reform movement. If bringing about change means injecting a productive level of stress and tension within traditional schools, so be it. We need to loosen the grip that stifles creativity and risk taking.

Managers bring conversations about the proper role, scope, and purpose of education. Managers bring policy making to the community, sparking discussion about how best to teach students. Managers cause teachers to think about where their talents and energies would be best devoted.

Working together provides opportunities to achieve results we are more likely to achieve together than alone. Use the language of "we" and "our" and "us." You and I alone cannot achieve what must be done. We must also embrace complexity and ambiguity. Building trust, organizing the effort, evaluating the results, and involving the community are all parts of leadership and management in a school environment.

Management teaches us that we need people who know about the challenges we face and that we need people with the power to act. People who are strong in leadership, technical, and human relations skills. People who are trusted by their employees to have the best interest of the students, teachers, and families at heart. People who will mold a diverse workforce into a cohesive, productive team. These people will empower and motivate employees to peak performance by communicating expectations, objectives, and goals for the school.

The awesome school uses collaboration as a tool of management. Collaboration is a process that gets people to work together in new ways. The process does not end but spawns new ventures. Management changes the way we work in urging us to move from competing to building consensus; from working alone to including others from a diversity of cultures, fields, and sectors; from thinking about activities, services, and programs to thinking about results and strategies; and from focusing on short-term accomplishments to demanding long-term results.

Management teaches us to acknowledge each person and benefit from his or her customs, languages, preferences, and powers. Power is always present and never equal. We should acknowledge and value the different types of power each person brings to our effort. We must not confuse the power to make something happen with the power to control others.

The awesome school will attain results by working individual-to-individual, individual-to-school, and school-to-community. This includes mutual respect, understanding, and trust at all levels. Also included in the awesome school mentality are cultural differences, diversity, perception, and power.

The awesome school will define desired results. This is a declaration of the accomplishment we want to make. The more specific, the better we'll know how we are progressing. Managers remind us to stop and look around, decide if we are succeeding, and continue on our course or correct it if needed. Desired results must be long-term, but also be short-term enough to produce achievements that sustain enthusiasm. Desired results must be concrete, attainable, and measurable. We need to know what we are trying to achieve and when our attempt is successful.

We all need a sense of humor to help us slog through the marshland. The ability to laugh at oneself and laugh with others relieves pressure and allows us to continue our work.

We need to keep an open mind. While realizing that some ideas might be wrong, we must reexamine our basic assumptions about what is right. When a teacher comes and says that he or she wants to teach chess in place of the basic math class, listen.

In the awesome school conflict is inevitable and, actually, highly desirable. Lack of conflict may indicate that issues are buried. But sure as there is mud in the marshland, these issues will surface. For success, conflict cannot be about right and wrong, it must be about difference. By not allowing conflict, we limit our ability to change.

Managers in the awesome school call for output and action. Leaders may review the mission and desired results. Both are necessary. Managers lay out an action plan, leaders consult existing research. Again, both are necessary.

Managers constantly seek feedback by listening and assessing the efforts. They ask, "Is the effort effective?" "Is the effort adequate?" "Is the effort efficient?" "What lessons have we learned?" Honest answers to these questions create opportunities for further change, refinements, and improved results.

Leaders say we must work at being adaptable and flexible. Adaptability is the capacity to adjust to major changes. Flexibility is the capacity to remain open to varied ways of organizing the school environment.

Managers look at conveying an image. Our image is crucial. It must grab the hearts of the people.

Managers take us down a road that is really a cloverleaf. We keep coming back to the beginning, each time building on and improving what we have been doing. We don't start over. We learn, refine, shift, include others, increase the scope of our effort, and move on. Each time the road brings us back to the beginning, as weary as we might feel, we start again.

The awesome school brings people together, enhances trust, understands a vision, sees desired results, resolves conflicts, supports the staff, evaluates the results, creates visibility, involves the community, and changes the system.

Joe Nathan wants schools to be different. Not different in his way only, but different in different ways. He knows the kind of education he prefers, but he also knows it's not for everyone. Therefore, if some schools are to have what he wants, others cannot.

Nathan has been crusading for choice for over thirty years. He helped start the St. Paul Open School in St. Paul, Minnesota, one of the few early public alternative schools that are still going strong. His quest for more flexible education began even earlier. Denied permission at age ten to be absent from school to hear a well-known writer speak about racial discrimination, he decided that "[s]chool was getting in the way of [his] learning" (Nathan 1999). Emphasize student-centered learning. Let students investigate topics on their own. Allow teachers to serve as guides rather than foundations of knowledge. Together use a hands-on role.

Difficulty in educating American students remains an ongoing problem. Attendance in schools is low, academic achievement is often below average, and the dropout rate remains high. However, in recent years communication brought about by a new breed of administrators who also have management skills has somewhat helped bridge the gap between the cultures in a school environment. Children are unique individuals and a child's culture and environmental background is what makes him or her unique. Managers as leaders have emerged to help foster this uniqueness.

Many educators, parents, and politicians embrace the management/ leadership concept because it appears to protect the educational institution and at the same time provide for fundamental reform and systematic restructuring. Management and leadership have the potential to shift power from the bureaucracies to the schools themselves, and ultimately to the individuals responsible for them—educators, parents, and individual students. Management and leadership, combining freedom, accountability, and competition are an important piece in redesigning and strengthening public education.

Schools under the leadership and management of a new breed of administrators are offering what parents have been requesting. In these schools:

- Parents are allowed to be integral members of the educational team.
- Curriculum promotes cultural competence and appreciates ethnic diversity (teaching the history, language, stories, and values of the culture).
- Instructional methods promote cooperation, interaction, and success for students.

- Assessment practices include alternative methods, which allow for cultural differences.
- A culture of oneness supports student growth.
- Policy making is sensitive to the perceptions and values of the community.
- Programs show clear-cut goals leading to improved academic performances.
- Teachers and administrators provide the extra support necessary for improved academic performance.
- Learning is promoted in collaboration, not isolation.
- Students receive the skills needed to meet the demands of a changing society with core essentials of the basics (reading, writing, mathematics, and reasoning), allowing students to become involved citizens and contributors to the community.

Schools under leadership and management administrators allow teachers to begin where children are, not at the front of a curriculum guide. Teachers and administrators accept and build upon the premise that students differ in important ways (interests, backgrounds, and learning styles).

Leaders and managers encourage teachers to engage students in instruction through different learning modalities by appealing to different interests and by using varied rates of instruction along with varied degrees of complexity.

Leaders and managers help teachers provide specific ways for each student to learn as deeply as possible and as quickly as possible, without assuming one student's roadmap for learning is identical to everyone else's. Students are held to high standards and come to believe that learning involves effort, risk, and personal triumph.

Teachers are encouraged to use flexible time frames, call upon a range of instructional strategies, and become partners with their students to shape the learning environment. They do not force-fit learners into a standard mold. These teachers are students of their students.

Managers and leaders are in touch with their teachers and students. They unconditionally accept both as they are and expect them to become all that they can be.

Sheldon Kopp once said, "In the long run, we get no more than we have been willing to risk giving." Managers and leaders must take risks. Because Billy Martin (second baseman and former manager of the New York Yankees and Minnesota Twins baseball teams) was often more famous for his battles than for his batting, most managers today may be loath to embrace Martin as their role model. Perhaps the world just wasn't ready for Billy Martin's management style during his lifetime. However, Martin followed a classic blueprint for leadership development: throughout his long, varied career, he sought out and learned from many mentors. He, in turn, loved to work with young players, teaching them and helping them live up to their potential. He analyzed every situation, planned his best strategy, and set out to win. If he made a mistake, he learned from it. All told, we can learn a lot from him.

Management and leadership are both important. Leadership complements management, it doesn't replace it. You need a solid balance of management and leadership skills to reach your greatest potential. Management provides the systems, structure, and controls the school needs to keep going. In fact, your educational organization would spin out of control without good management. Leadership is about vision and direction. Both are necessary.

Steven Covey once said, "To begin with the end in mind means to start with a clear understanding of your destination. It means to know where you are going so that you better understand where you are now, so that the steps you take are always in the right direction."

Educators who work in our nation's schools represent the conscience of a society because they shape the conditions under which future generations learn about themselves and their relationships to others in the world.

Managers and leaders are in a position to encourage educators, families, and community members to be aware of the need to reinvigorate the language, social relations, and politics of education. Managers and leaders are in a position to analyze how power shapes knowledge and how education can help students reconcile the seemingly opposing needs of freedom and solidarity.

It has become a cliché to say that these are precarious times for public schools. It is also a reality. On one hand, improving schools is the public's top priority. On the other, significant numbers of Americans are giving up on public schools. Today's parents, and, indeed, all voters, need to see signs of success if they are to support public education and public schools.

Our goal is to achieve results. Managers and leaders focus on results. In today's educational world we need to achieve significant results at a much faster pace than at any other time in history. Schools need to change. However, change is the most talked about and least acted upon concept in the school reform movement. If bringing about change means injecting a productive level of stress and tension within our schools, so be it. We need to loosen the grip that stifles creativity and risk taking. Discourses that disrupt are among the most powerful instruments of social change that we can use today.

The time has come for American education to move on toward solutions that will make a difference in the lives of students and their families.

Managers and leaders are demanding that parents, teachers, and students come together to make that difference.

> If you can imagine it, you can create it. If you can dream it, you can become it.
>
> —William Arthur Ward

References

Avery, G., and E. Baker. 1990. *Psychology at Work*. 2nd ed. New York: Prentice Hall.

Ballou, D., and M. Podgursky. 2001. "Defining Merit: Let the Market Decide." *Education Matters* 27 (3):16–25.

Barger, R., 2002. http://www.nd.edu/-rbarger/www7/goal2000.html (accessed May 5, 2002).

———. "Benjamin Rush." Online: www.nd.edu/rush.html (accessed May 5, 2002).

———. "Thomas Jefferson." Online: www.nd.edu/jefferson.html (accessed May 5, 2002).

Bass, B., and J. Stogdell. 1999. *Handbook of Leadership*. New York: Routledge.

Bennis, W. 1999. *Learning to Lead: A Workbook on Becoming a Leader*. New York: Addison Wesley.

Berliner, C. 2001. "Improving the Quality of the Teaching Force." *Educational Leadership* 58 (8): 6–10.

Boser, U. 2000. "A Picture of the Teacher Pipeline: Baccalaureate and Beyond." *Education Week* 19 (18): 16–17.

Butts, F., and L. Cremin. 1965. *A History of Education in American Culture*. New York: Holt, Rinehart, and Winston.

Cawell, B. 2002. Charters Anniversary. *Newsweek* 63 (1): 39-43.

———. 1999. "Accountability." *Education Week* 19 (5): 27.

Cremin, L. 1957. *The Republic and the School: Horace Mann on the Education of Free Men*. New York: Teachers College Press.

Dewey, J. 1934. *A Common Faith*. New Haven, Conn.: Yale University Press.

———. 1916. *Democracy and Education*. New York: Free Press.

Drucker, P. 2001. *Managing the Nonprofit Organization*. New York: Harper Business.

————. 1999. *Management Challenges for the Twenty-first Century.* New York: Harper Business.

Farkas, S., J. Johnson, and T. Foleno. 2000. *A Sense of Calling: Who Teaches and Why?* New York: Public Agenda.

Fenton, J. 1990. "Ways to Boost Your Business Performance." *Mandarin Business* 21 (3): 113.

Ferrechio, S., and J. Grotto. 2001. "Florida Teacher Shortage Rings Schools' Alarm Bells." *Miami Herald,* January 3, 1B.

Finn, C., and K. Madigan. 2001. "Removing the Barriers for Teacher Candidates." *Educational Leadership* 58 (8): 29–31, 36.

Firestien, R. 2001. *Leading on the Creative Edge.* Colorado Springs, Colo.: Pinon Press.

French, W. 1987. *The Personal Management Process: Human Resources, Administration and Development.* 6th ed. Boston: Houghton Mifflin.

Gardner, H. 1983. *Frames of Mind: A Theory of Multiple Intelligences.* New York: Basic Books.

Giroux, H. 1998. *Schooling and the Struggle for Public Life.* Minneapolis: University of Minnesota Press.

Havel, V. 1998. "The State of the Republic." *New York Review of Books,* June 2, 42–46.

Haycock, K. 1998. "Good Teaching Matters a Lot." *Thinking K–16* 3 (2): 3–5.

Hodgkenson, H. 1998. "Demographics of Diversity for the Twenty-first Century." *Education Digest* 64 (1): 4–7.

Kaye, H. 1997. "Education of Children with Disabilities." *Disability Statistics Abstracts* 19. San Francisco: Disability Statistics Center.

Keller, B. 2000. "Rethinking Retirement." *Education Week* 20 (13): 33.

Kotter, J. 1991. "What Leaders Really Do." In *The Best of the Harvard Business Review.* Cambridge, Mass.: Harvard University Press.

Line, P. 1996. "Home Schooling: Coming of Age." *Education Leadership* 54 (2): 163–167.

Marlow, B., and M. Page. 1999. "Making the Most of the Classroom Mosaic: A Constructivist Perspective." *Multicultural Education* 6 (4): 19–21.

Marshall, D. 1999. *The Four Elements of Successful Management.* New York: AMACOM Publishing.

Maslow, A. 1959. *Creativity in Self-Actualizing People.* New York: Harper and Row.

Nathan, J. 1999. Personal interview, January 19.

————. 1996. *Charter Schools.* San Francisco: Jossey-Bass.

Ornstein, A., and D. Levine. 1993. *Foundations of Education.* Boston: Houghton Mifflin.

Osborn, A. 1953. *Applied Imagination*. New York: Charles Scribner and Sons.

Predpall, D. 1994, May/June. "Developing Quality Improvement Processes for Consulting Engineering Firms." *Journal of Management in Engineering*, 30–31.

Raubenger, J., P. Rowe, P. Piper, and S. West. 1969. *The Development of Secondary Education*. New York: Macmillan.

Raven, B., and J. Ruben. 1976. *Social Psychology: People in Groups*. New York: John Wiley and Sons.

Ryan, K., and K. Bohlen. 1999. *Building Character in Schools*. New York: Harper.

Sears, D. 1988. *Social Psychology*. 6th ed. New York: Prentice Hall.

Sergiovanni, T. 1996. *Leadership for the Schoolhouse*. Neadham Heights, Mass.: Allyn and Bacon.

Sterman, J. 1995. *The Systems Thinker*. New York: Harcourt.

Tell, C. 2001. "Responses." *Educational Leadership* 58 (8): 18–19.

Vecchio, R., G. Hearn, and G. Southey. 1988. *Organizational Behavior: Life at Work in Australia*. Sydney: Harcourt Brace.

Wolk, R. 2001. "Alternative Answers." *Teacher Magazine* 12 (January): 4.

Woodward, C. 1969. *The Manual Training School*. New York: Arno Press and New York Times.

About the Author

Darlene Leiding is an expert in the realm of charter schools and alternative education and has used her experience to create an elementary and high school alternative program operating within the Minneapolis Public Schools contracted alternative system. She was also responsible for bringing Heart of the Earth Center for American Indian Education Charter School, located in Minneapolis, Minnesota, out of financial and academic difficulties. She has accepted a position with the administrative team at Urban Academy Charter School, located in St. Paul, Minnesota. She is also the author of *The Won't Learners: An Answer to Their Cry* (ScarecrowEducation, 2002).